HOLLYWOOD
DREAMS MADE REAL

HOLLYWOOD DREAMS MADE REAL

Irving Thalberg and the Rise of M-G-M

MARK A. VIEIRA

ABRAMS, NEW YORK

TO THE MEMORY OF MY MOTHER AND FATHER —M.A.V.

Editor: Elisa Urbanelli
Art Director: Michelle Ishay
Designers: Mumtaz Mustafa and Laura Klynstra
Production Manager: Jules Thomson

Library of Congress Cataloging-in-Publication Data

Vieira, Mark A., 1950-
Hollywood dreams made real : Irving Thalberg and the rise of M-G-M / by
Mark A. Vieira.
    p. cm.
ISBN 978-0-8109-7234-6 (Harry N. Abrams, inc.)
1. Thalberg, Irving G., 1899-1936. 2. Motion picture producers and
directors—United States—Biography. 3. Metro-Goldwyn-Mayer. I.
Title.
 PN1998.3.T467V54 2008
 791.4302'3092—dc22
 [B]
                                                    2008017547

Published in 2008 by Abrams, an imprint of Harry N. Abrams, Inc.
All rights reserved. No portion of this book may be reproduced, stored in
a retrieval system, or transmitted in any form or by any means, mechani-
cal, electronic, photocopying, recording, or otherwise, without written
permission from the publisher.

Printed and bound in China
10 9 8 7 6 5 4 3 2 1

Abrams books are available at special discounts when purchased in
quantity for premiums and promotions as well as fundraising or
educational use. Special editions can also be created to specification.
For details, contact specialmarkets@hnabooks.com or the address below.

HNA
harry n. abrams, inc.
a subsidiary of La Martinière Groupe
115 West 18th Street
New York, NY 10011
www.hnabooks.com

Page 1: The Yellow Room set in *Grand Hotel*. Photograph by Clarence Bull

Page 2: *Grand Hotel*'s stars, clockwise from upper left: Greta Garbo, John Barrymore, Joan Crawford, Lionel Barrymore, Jean Hersholt, Lewis Stone, and Wallace Beery. Photo montage by Clarence Bull

Endpapers: A set reference still of the Capulet gardens built for *Romeo and Juliet* on Stage 15 at M-G-M.

CONTENTS

PREFACE

If you have ever listened to Tarzan's jungle yell, seen Jean Harlow slink across a satin boudoir, heard Charles Laughton cry out "Mr. Christian!" or watched Greta Garbo stride through the lobby of the Grand Hotel, you have seen the work of Irving Thalberg. Did you know that he made the motion pictures in which these scenes appear? If you don't, it isn't your fault. Thalberg made more than four hundred films. He put his name on none of them. "Credit you give yourself," said Thalberg, "isn't worth having." *Tarzan the Ape Man, China Seas, Mutiny on the Bounty,* and *Grand Hotel* are nominally orphans, popular art created without a signature. Unlike the typical Hollywood producer, Thalberg was not interested in flinging his name at the public. He was interested in making films—films that would entertain, enlighten, and evoke emotion.

That Thalberg accomplished these goals was demonstrated by the phenomenal success of Metro-Goldwyn-Mayer. He cofounded the company in 1924 with a small-time producer named Louis B. Mayer. Thalberg's gift for filmmaking and Mayer's knack for management combined to make M-G-M the greatest studio in the history of the world. Yet Thalberg remained a shadowy, enigmatic figure. He was better known as the husband of movie star Norma Shearer than as the prime architect of the Hollywood studio system. When he died in 1936, at the age of thirty-seven, the mythmaking began. F. Scott Fitzgerald made him the subject of *The Last Tycoon.* The Academy of Motion Picture Arts and Sciences named an award after him. The Irving G.

Thalberg Memorial Award is not presented yearly; only when the Academy's Board of Directors wishes to honor a producer whose work reflects "a consistently high quality of motion picture production." The Thalberg Award has been given to, among others, Walt Disney, Alfred Hitchcock, Billy Wilder, and Warren Beatty.

Irving Grant Thalberg was born in Brooklyn on May 30, 1899. He was a frail child, ravaged by a siege of childhood diseases. Doctors predicted that he would die by thirty. Confinement to a sickroom gave him the chance to read literary classics of every country and tradition. By the time he had recovered sufficiently to enter the work force, he had the mind and vocabulary of a scholar. His frail constitution limited his work options, but, pushed by an ambitious mother and pulled by a friendly neighbor, young Irving joined the film industry. The neighbor was Carl Laemmle, president of Universal Pictures. In less than two years, Thalberg's insight and self-confidence had elevated him to the executive level. Why should he fear bureaucrats when he had stared down death?

Beginning with *The Hunchback of Notre Dame*, Thalberg brought his literary favorites to the silver screen. When he had gotten all he could from aesthetically limited Universal, Thalberg joined Louis B. Mayer. A happy partnership led them to found M-G-M. Within three years, they had made it the most successful studio in Hollywood. For twelve years almost every M-G-M film bore Thalberg's imprint. His shrewdness and ingenuity broke new ground in filmmaking. He innovated story conferences, sneak previews, and extensive retakes. He introduced the horror film and coauthored the "Production Code." He achieved a synthesis of theater and film. He made stars of Lon Chaney, Ramon Novarro, John Gilbert, Joan Crawford, Clark Gable, Helen Hayes, Jean Harlow, Marie Dressler, Wallace Beery, and Greta Garbo.

By the time Thalberg was thirty-five, he was acknowledged as the greatest producer in Hollywood. His films, a rare blend of taste and commercialism, were honored with awards and ratified by box-office returns. Then, as he stood poised to lead the film community to new horizons, his doctors' prophecies came true. Thalberg died, leaving a widow, two children—and an impressive legacy. Films that had enlightened, entertained, and evoked emotion would also endure.

Hollywood films were never intended to endure. They were printed on an unstable cellulose nitrate base, shipped to theaters near and far, and then stripped of their silver content. No one expected a film to be of interest after it had finished its engagements. "Making pictures is not like writing literature or composing music or painting masterpieces," wrote the *Los Angeles*

Times columnist Edwin Schallert in 1934. "The screen story is essentially a thing of today and once it has had its run, that day is finished. So far there has never been a classic film in the sense that there is a classic novel or poem or canvas or sonata. Last year's picture, however strong its appeal at the time, is a book that has gone out of circulation." You are reading this book because Mr. Schallert and his contemporaries were wrong. Thalberg's films refused to go out of circulation.

Patrons of American movie theaters—your parents, grandparents, and great-grandparents—told the owners of those theaters that they wanted to see *The Big Parade, Ben-Hur, Min and Bill, Grand Hotel,* and *The Good Earth* again. And again. By the mid-1950s the reissue was a common practice. Then came television. M-G-M sold its film library to TV, spawning the *Early Show* and the *Late Show*. Actors who had stood petrified before microphones in the first talking pictures could now judge themselves from a living-room sofa. The real judging was done by the millions of Americans who owned television sets. It was this mass of consumers that voted to preserve Thalberg's work. Beginning in 1957, more people saw Thalberg movies than had ever seen them in initial release. They saw them on TV in the 1950s, in revival houses in the 1960s, on college campuses in the 1970s, on videocassettes in the 1980s, and on cable TV in the 1990s. In the twenty-first century we have DVDs and the Internet. It is possible to go to a computer at any time of the day or night and track down a Thalberg film.

After I view a Thalberg film on Turner Classic Movies (TCM), I instinctively and habitually want more. There is, of course, the Internet Movie Database, but I want more than just facts. I want to keep something of the experience. Those shimmering images are fleeting and evanescent. Only if they were captured by on-the-set still photographers or approximated by skilled portrait photographers is some aspect of them made tangible—and collectible. Just as we take photos of friends in a school play, M-G-M took pictures of its players. These "stills" were made to sell the movie. They did that, but they were meant to be discarded afterward. Fortunately for us, they were not. Seventy-five years later, they give us access to the exotic, magical world that Thalberg created. After seeing a Thalberg film, these photographs are what I seek.

In *Hollywood Dreams Made Real*, I have assembled an album of photographs from Thalberg's films. This book is not intended to be, nor can it be, a conventional biography. Thalberg deserves a full-scale biography, one that details previously unexamined aspects of his professional, political, and personal lives, and one that dispels the foolish and sometimes hostile apocrypha that have formed around his legend. I am preparing that book. In the meantime, using some of the unseen documents and unpublished photos I found for it, I have created this companion volume. This is a visual survey of the Thalberg era, with highlights of his achievements. It is also intended as a companion to the Thalberg films exhibited on TCM and released on DVD by Warner Home Video.

There is another reason for doing a book of this type. For all his fascination with Broadway plays, Thalberg told his stories visually. The great moments in his films stay in the memory as much for their use of screen grammar, for their dynamic composition, and for their interplay of light and shadow as for their content. More than any other producer or any other studio, Thalberg and M-G-M manipulated lenses, filters, and lighting instruments to affect the viewer subjectively. Think of the springtime love scene in Thalberg's first M-G-M film, *He Who Gets Slapped*. Director Victor Seastrom and cameraman Milton Moore could have made an effective scene in any backlit meadow, but they specifically chose an area where the noon light would create a moving pattern of feathery shadows over the entire scene. Seastrom then played the realistic elements of the scene against this suggestive background, gradually having the hypnotic movement of the shadows dominate the scene, just as Norma Shearer and John Gilbert were being dominated by their own emotions, both in the scene and in real life.

Most of Thalberg's films contain moments such as these, in which cinematic technique transcends mere exposition and gives the viewer something to treasure. Thalberg could not have accomplished this without the skill, the inventiveness, and the genius of his collaborators. There have been books about M-G-M cameramen (George Folsey, Harold Rosson, and William Daniels), about M-G-M portrait photographers (Ruth Harriet Louise, Clarence Sinclair Bull, and George Hurrell), and, of course, about "Thalberg directors" (Victor Seastrom, King Vidor, and George Cukor). There has never been a book comprising the visual achievements of these artists under Thalberg.

I have arranged these images and related these stories in a pictorial history format. I believe that you will be able to understand these films more fully if you can see them in chronological order. It does make a difference that Joan Crawford was playing a "dancing daughter" in 1928 and a "glamorous socialite" in 1935—and not the other way around. Thalberg groomed Crawford for stardom, and it took time. I want to show how he made her the unique star that she was. I can only do that by presenting the stages of that process in strict chronology. I recommend that you begin at the beginning, and stroll with me through the gates of the company that gave America a new folklore. Before Thalberg, there was no Grand Hotel in the American consciousness. In visiting the Grand Hotel, or any setting created in an M-G-M film between 1924 and 1936, you will travel to a time and place defined by one remarkable filmmaker, Irving Grant Thalberg.

Irving Grant Thalberg, the vice president in charge of production at Metro-Goldwyn-
Mayer Studios, in 1932, at the age of thirty-three. Photograph by Russell Ball

Carl Laemmle had just made the youthful Irving Thalberg general manager of Universal City when they posed for this 1920 photograph. Most Universal employees called Laemmle "Uncle Carl." Thalberg called him "C.L."

I ‖ THE BOY WONDER

UNIVERSAL CITY

Irving Thalberg's meteoric arc over Hollywood began in New York City. After frustrating stints in his grandfather's department store and several shipping firms, the brainy nineteen-year-old found a job at 1600 Broadway, the office of Universal Pictures. Even though the president of Universal, Carl Laemmle, was his grandmother's neighbor, Thalberg had applied for the job without currying favor. He was not attending college because his mother, Henrietta Heyman Thalberg, feared that the required load of courses would be too heavy for his fragile constitution. He had been born with cyanosis and diagnosed as a "blue baby" with a rheumatic heart. Doctors predicted at first that he would not survive his twentieth birthday. At sixteen he was stricken with rheumatic fever, and his heart was further damaged. If he was very lucky, said the doctors, he might live to thirty, but no more than that. That he survived his teens was due to his mother's diligence—and to his own sense of destiny. He approached adulthood with a determination to make the most of every opportunity and to use what time remained in the most efficacious manner. Thus motivated, he became Carl Laemmle's assistant within a few months.

Laemmle's film-producing studio was not in New York, New Jersey, or Long Island, but in California's San Fernando Valley. It was called Universal City. In late 1919, Laemmle took young Thalberg to the sprawling property. Henrietta and William Thalberg were distressed to see their son leave home for the first time, but Laemmle needed help. Universal City was not making enough films, and those it was releasing were poor. Once there, Laemmle demoted a few employees and then suddenly decamped to New York, leaving Thalberg at the studio with a triumvirate of managers. "I need someone to keep an eye on things for me," said Laemmle. He got more than he bargained for. Thalberg, having schooled himself in William James's philosophy of pragmatism, took a look at the loafers who were fighting among themselves and planned his strategy.

"It was one of those periods when people were getting fired right and left," Thalberg later recounted. "I took charge because there was no one left to take charge." The slight young man whom illness had deprived of physical power took the first opportunity to seize corporate power. "In a business where no one had the courage of his own convictions," he later said, "I knew I was right that I should make them do it my way." When Laemmle returned, Thalberg wondered if the elfish fifty-three-year-old would fire him. Laemmle surprised him.

"I would like that you should stay here," Laemmle said. "You are completely in charge of the studio." On May 30, 1920, Thalberg turned twenty-one. He was earning $450 a week as general manager of Universal City.* So began the career of the "Boy Wonder of Hollywood."

The unexpected success of Stroheim's films prompted Universal to gamble on bigger productions. Sets under construction at Universal City in this 1922 photograph include the Monte Carlo plaza for *Foolish Wives* and the cathedral for *The Hunchback of Notre Dame*. Universal produced nearly two hundred films a year, a modest assortment of melodramas, serials, westerns, and comedies.

The City of Streets
Universal Studio
Universal City Calif.

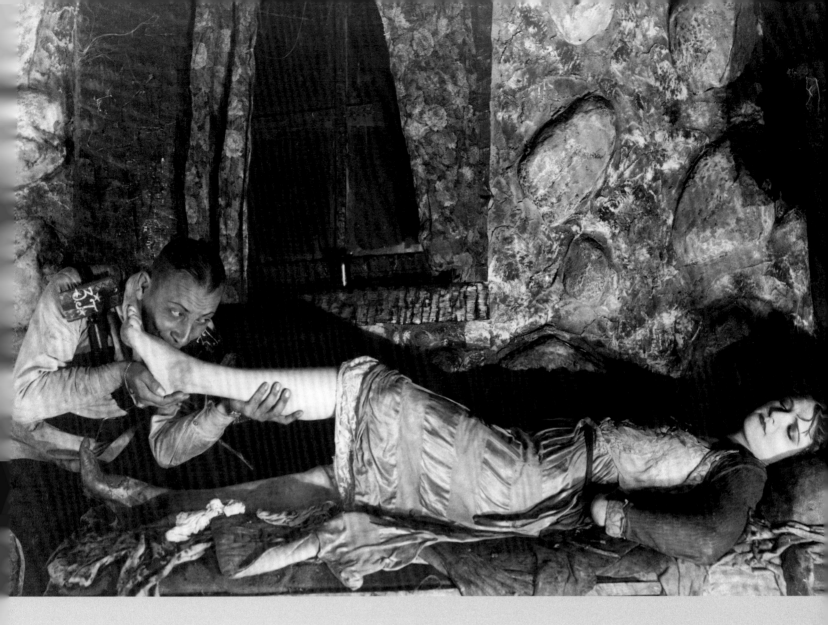

As both director and star of Universal's *Foolish Wives* (1922), Erich von Stroheim introduced the American public to a character who was fascinating and repellent, a "swanking, swaggering scion of militarism with all the absurd vanities, the ugly hypocrisies, the silly affectations of the kulturist." His costar in *Foolish Wives* was an actress billed simply (and pretentiously) as "Miss DuPont." Thalberg looked askance at Stroheim. "Von

Stroheim was terribly, terribly slow," recalled cinematographer William Daniels in 1968. "There would be constant rehearsal. He would select 'types,' too, for parts, rather than accomplished actors or actresses. It was his job—and he was proud of that—to be more or less a Svengali, to turn the 'types' into 'great performers.' That took a terrible lot of time, endless time."

This Monte Carlo set, erected for *Foolish Wives,* was not the largest yet built in Hollywood, but, thanks to Stroheim's mania for realism, it was needlessly expensive. Thalberg made Hollywood history when he fired Stroheim from his next film, *Merry-Go-Round,* challenging for the first time the primacy of the director. Because of Thalberg, producers took control of the filmmaking process, and autocratic directors such as Stroheim, D. W. Griffith, and Rex Ingram went out of fashion.

15

A novel that Thalberg read in a Brooklyn sickbed became a Universal production eight years later. *The Hunchback of Notre Dame* was one of 1923's biggest hits and made a star of Lon Chaney, seen here with Nigel De Brulier.

Irving Thalberg made a lasting impression on screen-writer Lenore Coffee when she came to his office for advice one day in 1920. "On leaving the studio," she wrote years later, "I kept thinking back on what a remarkable young man he was. Although barely twenty-one, he had enormous dignity. I couldn't imagine anyone taking a liberty with him, either in business or in his per-sonal life." Yet, by the middle of 1922, Thalberg found himself frustrated by Carl Laemmle. The amiable mogul wanted Thalberg to marry his daughter Rosabelle but would not give the "Boy Genius" a raise. Thalberg liked Rosabelle, but not enough to slow his career. The ambi-tious young man began to seek a better situation.

Louis B. Mayer's success in Los Angeles underwrote a hand-some new structure for his offices, built in the style of the château of Chenonceaux. To make ends meet, he rented space to independent producer B. P. Schulberg.

3800 MISSION ROAD

In late 1922 there were numerous studios for which Irving Thalberg could have left Universal. The Fox Film Corporation, Metro Pictures, or Goldwyn would have been options. Hollywood's "Big Two," Famous Players-Lasky and First National, had turned down Thalberg. Jesse Lasky and Joseph Schenck both thought he looked too boyish and wanted too much money. Thalberg had a booster in Edwin Loeb, who was Carl Laemmle's attorney. Loeb felt badly for the conscientious young man but lacked contacts at the big studios. He did know a small studio on the outskirts of East Los Angeles, so he arranged a meeting between Thalberg and thirty-eight-year-old Louis B. Mayer. When the short, muscular Mayer came bounding into Loeb's Wilshire district living room one Sunday in November, Thalberg immediately recognized him. He had seen him on November 11, 1918—Armistice Day—in front of the Strand Theater in New York. Mayer had been feverishly decorating the theater with posters for his first production *Virtuous Wives*, completely ignoring the celebration rushing past him. The image had stayed with Thalberg. Four years later, he was asking this single-minded entrepreneur for a job. If he got the job, it would be a step down from Universal.

Louis B. Mayer Productions was located not in Hollywood but northeast of downtown Los Angeles. He was renting space from a declining studio called Selig Polyscope. Its founder, Colonel William Selig,

had converted most of his property into the Selig Zoo, the country's largest private collection of exotic animals. "Louis B. chose the Selig Zoo because it was the cheapest place in town," Hedda Hopper wrote years later. "That was a funny lot, with wild animals roaming around just like the actors. The lions and tigers were toothless and tame, but if you didn't know that, it was rather frightening, coming 'round a corner and suddenly running into one." Mayer produced five films a year, mostly featuring his one star, a modestly talented blonde named Anita Stewart. He shared his studio with a producer named B. P. Schulberg. "When the Schulbergs and the Mayers arrived as part of the movie rush of the early Twenties," wrote Budd Schulberg, "Mission Road was still what its name implied: a narrow, winding rural road that led from the little Spanish church in the Plaza to the mission in the open fields. The primitive Selig-Mayer-Schulberg studio with its dirty white stucco walls and its small silent stages looked across to two adjoining wonders, the Alligator Farm and Gay's Ostrich Farm." What did this setup have to offer the ambitious young Thalberg?

Mayer's company was small, but he had an elegant new office building, a sufficient number of stages, and a steady output of films made by talented directors such as John Stahl and Marshall Neilan. Mayer also had excellent distribution outlets with First National and Metro

Five years before he adopted Leo the Lion, Louis B. Mayer had an American eagle for a mascot and a studio on the grounds of the Selig Zoo in East Los Angeles. He had immigrated to America from Russia via Nova Scotia, and even when he changed his birth date to July 4, no one stopped to ask where he had come from. "The word 'pioneer' has a tiresome ring, but that's what Mr. Mayer was," Norma Shearer wrote years later. "He had tremendous energy and courage. If he hadn't set up shop next to the Selig Zoo, I might still be in Montreal, giving music lessons to some brat who was kicking the hell out of a piano."

Pictures. He could offer Thalberg a subsidiary producing company and 20 percent of the profits, if his distributors would okay the deal. This was all attractive to Thalberg. The key element of Louis B. Mayer Productions was Mayer himself. For a student of human nature such as Thalberg, Mayer was a fascinating specimen.

Lazar Meher was born in the Ukraine in July 1884. Anti-Semitism drove his family to St. John, New Brunswick, where his father, Jacob, ran a scrap-iron business and his mother, Sarah, ran a dry-goods store. While still a teenager, Mayer used his biceps, his fists, and his gift of gab to build his own salvage company. Its profits enabled him to buy into nickelodeons and then into movie theaters, and eventually to extend a film exchange along the eastern seaboard. While in Haverhill, Massachusetts, with his wife and two young daughters, he leased the state's rights to the general release of D. W. Griffith's *The Birth of a Nation*. It was the birth of his fortune. Even so, he came to see that the real money in moving pictures lay not in exhibiting them but in producing them. The idea of manufacturing a product that he could sell, yet still own, fascinated him. And

he could control its quality. "I will make only pictures that I won't be ashamed to have my children see," said Mayer. "I'm determined that my little Edie and my little Irene will never be embarrassed. And they won't be if all my pictures are moral and clean." In early 1919, he had decided that California was the place to make such pictures.

Mayer's distributors would not allow him to create a subsidiary production unit for Thalberg, but Mayer was determined to hire him. Mayer was convinced that this serious young man could lift his company to the level of the larger studios. By the same token, Thalberg saw in Mayer a remarkable energy and an uncanny business sense. On February 15, 1923, Louis B. Mayer Productions hired Irving Thalberg, creating the post of vice president in charge of production. His starting salary was $500 a week. "Find your way around," Mayer told Thalberg. "A man must crawl before he walks, and walk before he runs."

One of Thalberg's first goals for Mayer Productions was to find an actress to groom for stardom in case Anita Stewart should leave. Thalberg had someone in mind. While he was still at Universal, Sam Marx, his friend in the New York office, had recommended a twenty-year-old Canadian girl named Norma Shearer. She had begun her career in moving pictures by playing piano in theaters, modeling for artists, appearing in tire advertisements, and doing extra work; all this in defiance of Griffith, who told her that she was too odd looking to appear on film. Thalberg had looked at her work, made an offer, and been refused. Maybe it was time to try again.

In the first week of March, Shearer and her mother, Edith, found themselves at 3800 Mission Road. "We were sitting in the reception room," recalled Shearer, "when a very polite and modest young office boy came through a small swinging gate. He held it open for us, smiled, and said nothing. In we went. We found ourselves in Mr. Mayer's office. To our amazement the young man went around the big desk and sat down behind it. . . . We soon suspected that the young man who had greeted us could not be an office boy. And indeed we soon learned that he was Irving G. Thalberg, Hollywood's so-called Boy Wonder."

Mayer and Thalberg signed Shearer to a five-year contract with six-month options and began loaning her out to other studios so that she could be trained in the art of film acting—at someone else's expense. The plan worked. Within a year, Shearer was becoming known as a Mayer Productions player. More importantly, Thalberg's studious, methodical approach to film production was elevating the quality of Mayer's films and allowing for Mayer's taste. "If a story makes me cry," said Mayer, "I know it's good." Tears were shed in theaters but not in accounting offices. Thalberg was making money for Mayer, so much that the great Marcus Loew, owner of the Loew's theater chain, grew curious enough to visit the quaint Mission Road complex. Mayer gave the magnate the grand tour and a grand speech. "When you stop to think about it," expounded Mayer, "all producers use the same raw stock, the same make of camera, the same textures in sets, the same textiles in costumes, the same lighting equipment. It's all the same. There's only one way a producer can be different." Mayer touched his forefinger to his forehead. "Brains!"

Loew got the message. He owned Metro Pictures, and if the people who were running it had brains, they were not using them. They had foolishly let Rudolph Valentino go after making him a star. Now Metro was in trouble. By the end of 1923, it was obvious to Loew and the rest of the film industry that Thalberg was accomplishing far more than Mayer had hoped he would. He was putting Mayer—and himself—in a position to grab the brass ring.

Mayer was in early middle age when he gambled on a move to Los Angeles. To his secretary Florence Browning, he was a "funny little man, riding around in a Ford, telling everyone confidently that he was going to be the greatest man in the picture-making business. He seemed to have absolutely no reticence, no inhibitions, no sense of embarrassment at his evident manifestations of conceit."

Marcus Loew's theater chain was always in need of films. If one company could not supply them, perhaps a combination of companies could.

Twenty-three-year-old Irving Thalberg made an indelible impression on Norma Shearer and her mother on their first day at Mission Road.

"Did you see those eyes?" Edith Shearer asked her daughter.

"I should say I did," replied Shearer.

"What eyes!"

"Wouldn't it be wonderful if you married that nice young man!" said Edith.

Shearer was too awestruck to answer.

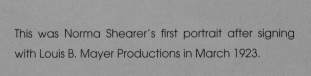

This was Norma Shearer's first portrait after signing with Louis B. Mayer Productions in March 1923.

The quiet dignity of the Goldwyn plant would soon be supplanted
by the happy hum of Metro-Goldwyn employees. This photograph
shows the Washington Boulevard entrance.

10202 WASHINGTON BOULEVARD

Thalberg learned at Universal that a film never started shooting until it had been properly prepared. This meant story conferences, rewriting, and more conferences. This system had been initiated by pioneer producer Thomas Ince several years earlier and adopted by Thalberg at Universal City. It was practical at a large facility that had the luxury of shooting numerous films simultaneously. It was not practical at Mission Road. As Thalberg took more time over each film, Mayer watched his stages stand empty. Only four films were released in 1923. They were well written, well made, and well received, but they were not enough for Mayer; he needed more. "Think big," he would say. "That's the path of the future." Then he would look at the big studios in Hollywood and declare that he and Irving could handle any of them. He had, in fact, been Metro's secretary for a time, so he knew something. Ever the diplomat, he had maintained a friendship with a Metro attorney named J. Robert Rubin. Mayer knew that Rubin had recently moved to Loew's, Incorporated, and could share information with him.

Exhibition magnate Marcus Loew had a problem. He owned more than one hundred theaters, primarily in big cities. The Loew's chain constantly needed films. Loew had bought Metro three years earlier in the hope that the modest Hollywood studio would keep his chain supplied, but Metro's managers failed to make enough films. Loew was thinking of dumping Metro when the head of another production company approached him. Frank Godsol was managing the splendid Culver City plant known as the Goldwyn Company. The distinction of *Company* was important. Godsol had ousted the company's founder Samuel Goldwyn but retained his name. At this point, the name was worth less than the founder. Without the leadership of the temperamental but farsighted Goldwyn, the company was drifting. The theatrical impresario Lee Shubert may have envisioned a merger when he introduced Godsol to Loew. There is no record of how the idea was born or at what point Mayer became an element of it, but in December 1923, Loew looked at three struggling companies and saw the potential for a merger.

In January 1924 Loew instructed his executive officer Nicholas Schenck to meet with Godsol, Rubin, Mayer, and Thalberg about the possibility of a merger. Loew wanted to combine: (1) Metro's small stable of talent and excellent distribution system; (2) Goldwyn's large stable of talent and immense physical plant; and (3) Mayer's management skills. In short order, Loew made his move. He dissolved Metro, and then paid $4.7 million for the Goldwyn Company and $76,500 for Mayer's company. To get a clear title to Goldwyn, he paid $600,000 to buy out Sam Goldwyn's stock. Loew felt that his capital entitled him to place his own son at the head of the new combine. This would have meant displacing Thalberg with Arthur Loew. Mayer stood fast, insisting that Thalberg be production head. A year of working together had not only inspired affection between Mayer and Thalberg but also demonstrated what Thalberg could accomplish with even the most ordinary material. Impressed by Mayer's loyalty, Loew agreed.

The new company was named Metro-Goldwyn. Neither Thalberg's nor Mayer's name was included in the merger hyphenate, but the title card of each film would include the legend: "Louis B. Mayer Presents." Thalberg declined credit, contenting himself with the title of vice president in charge of production and a weekly salary of $650. Mayer was vice president and general manager, earning $1,500 a week. Completing the "Mayer Group" was Rubin, who would remain in New York to function as a link with the "Loew's Group." The Mayer Group partners would also receive 20 per-

cent of the net profits of each film produced; 10 percent to Mayer, 5 percent to Thalberg, and 5 percent to Rubin. Their yearly release quota was set at fifteen films. Since Loew now owned 111 theaters, the new company was responsible for filling 250,000 theater seats weekly, a big task by any standards.

The merger became official on April 10, 1924, when Mayer and Thalberg signed a fourteen-page contract. On April 26, 1924, the new company hosted a grand-opening ceremony on the lawn of its Culver City studio. Mayer and Thalberg chose to retain the Goldwyn mascot, a lion. The fierce beast eventually acquired the name Leo. "From my new dressing room," recalled Norma Shearer, "I could see the brightly lighted sign above the studio. Leo became, for me, a symbol of the courage of these men in undertaking so brave a venture."

METRO PICTURES CORPORATION

Location: 1325 Eleanor Avenue, Hollywood

Management: In disarray following abrupt resignation of founder Richard Rowland

Facility: More executive offices than stages

Directors: Rex Ingram, Victor Schertzinger

Players: Ramon Novarro, Monte Blue, Alice Lake

Releasing films for: Mae Murray, Buster Keaton, Jackie Coogan

Assets: $3.1 million

SAMUEL GOLDWYN PRODUCTIONS

Location: 10202 Washington Boulevard, Culver City
Built by Thomas Ince in 1915

Management: Frank Godsol, Abraham Lehr

Facility: Forty-six acres, six glass-walled stages, dozens of outdoor sets, a three-story administration building, writer's offices, editing rooms, screening rooms, dressing rooms, carpentry shops, lumber sheds, paint shops, and a restaurant

Directors: Marshall Neilan, King Vidor, Erich von Stroheim, Charles Brabin, Victor Seastrom

Players: Aileen Pringle, John Gilbert, Blanche Sweet, Conrad Nagel, Eleanor Boardman, William Haines

Releasing films for: Marion Davies

Assets: $4.7 million (including an interest in New York's Capitol Theater, the world's largest movie theater)

LOUIS MAYER PRODUCTIONS

Location: 3800 Mission Road, Los Angeles

Management: Louis B. Mayer, Irving G. Thalberg

Facility: Miniscule

Directors: John Stahl, Reginald Barker, Fred Niblo

Players: Norma Shearer, Barbara La Marr, Anita Stewart, Mildred Harris Chaplin

Assets: $0.5 million

Louis B. Mayer (left) and Irving Thalberg (right) visited director Reginald Barker on the set of *The Dixie Handicap*. "Mayer insisted that he and Irving were 'brothers under the skin,'" recalled Frances Marion. "Nobody ever skinned them to find out, but on prima facie they were opposite as the two poles." Mayer was robust, emotional, and extroverted; Thalberg was slight, thoughtful, and reserved. Their complementary natures made the Metro-Goldwyn studio an instant success. The one cloud hovering over the new studio was anxiety over Thalberg's damaged heart. "If only he were healthy," Mayer confided to his wife and daughters. He did not know that Thalberg spent late nights courting the effervescent actress Constance Talmadge.

II A QUIET LION

1924

The merger of three Hollywood companies into Metro-Goldwyn Studios (and Metro-Goldwyn-Mayer Releasing) created three hundred jobs. It also cost a few, as Louis B. Mayer and his new studio manager, J. J. Cohn, took charge. "The grafters and the incompetents went first," wrote Irene Mayer Selznick, "then the trouble-makers and the uncooperatives." Among the dispossessed were Goldwyn boss Abraham Lehr and Metro boss Joe Engel. "Strangely enough," wrote Selznick, "out-and-out enemies were not fired—not if they were talented." Directors Marshall Neilan and Erich von Stroheim remained, in spite of earlier conflicts with Irving Thalberg. It was a hopeful, exuberant period, and grudges were put aside. "Everything was very exciting during that time," wrote screenwriter Lenore Coffee. "There was a great hegira over to the old Goldwyn studios. We all lived in a state of euphoria. Louis B. Mayer was beaming on everyone."

While Mayer, Cohn, and supervisor Harry Rapf organized the physical plant, Thalberg got the lifeblood of the company pumping—stories. "The first thing Irving did after the merger," wrote Coffee, "was to inaugurate Saturday morning meetings. There were discussions of what films we had seen during the week, which ones were doing good business, and why. It was really like someone holding a seminar. Thalberg felt that our sole aim in life was to find out why some films could tune into the audience and why others could not."

Along with writers, directors, and supervisors, Metro-Goldwyn inherited projects from Goldwyn and Metro.

Hobart Henley's *Sinners in Silk* was the first film to start shooting on the new studio lot, but it was essentially a Goldwyn project, just as Victor Schertzinger's *Bread* was a Metro adoptee. By mid-year, the local press was referring to the new studio not by its two-name hyphenate but by the name of its releasing company. This was shortened further to the catchy "M-G-M."

Thalberg needed to initiate the first true Metro-Goldwyn-Mayer film, one planned, filmed, and released by the new company. For this auspicious project, he drew on a play he had seen in New York two years earlier. The Theatre Guild's production of Leonid Andreyev's *He Who Gets Slapped* starred Richard Bennett as a disgraced scientist who hides his disappointment behind clown makeup. Thalberg knew the perfect actor to portray this wretched character. Lon Chaney was riding high on the success of *The Hunchback of Notre Dame*, a project Thalberg had guided before leaving Universal. Thalberg matched the awesomely talented Chaney with the intuitive Swedish director Victor Sjöström (working in Hollywood as Seastrom), and then cast Norma Shearer as the circus rider whom the clown secretly loves. To round out the cast, Thalberg chose a young actor who had cut his teeth at the old Ince Studios in Santa Monica as a writer, a director, and finally as an actor. John Gilbert was twenty-six, fiery, and full of enthusiasm for M-G-M. "It's so great to be a part of anything like this," he said. "I just can't believe I'm really here." Thalberg's casting of *He Who Gets Slapped* was more than auspicious, for each of its players would become part of Metro-Goldwyn-Mayer's mythology.

"Here is the truth about today's flappers and lounge lizards!" promised the ads for *Sinners in Silk*, the first film to start shooting on the Metro-Goldwyn lot. It went before the cameras on the historic date of April 30, 1924, but it was not the company's first production; it was a leftover Goldwyn project. "Producers discovered that the best way to turn a weak picture into a hit was to put 'sin,' 'sex,' or 'sinner' in the title," wrote Adolphe Menjou. "In *Sinners in Silk*, I played a fifty-year-old widower who gets rejuvenated with new glands and courts a girl half his age." In this scene are Eleanor Boardman as a flapper, Bradley Ward as a lounge lizard, and Hedda Hopper as a reformed Victorian.

Circe the Enchantress was one of numerous 1924 films distributed by Metro-Goldwyn's releasing arm, Metro-Goldwyn-Mayer, but not made by the new studio. It was a Tiffany production starring Mae Murray and directed by her husband, Robert Z. Leonard. Before long, Murray and Leonard would dissolve Tiffany and work directly for Metro-Goldwyn.

After being fired from Universal by Thalberg, Erich von Stroheim went to the Goldwyn Company, which inexplicably allowed him to film Frank Norris's grim "American naturalist" novel *McTeague* without supervision. Stroheim changed the title to *Greed* and had Zasu Pitts portray the gold-obsessed Trina and Gibson Gowland the brutish McTeague in real-life locations. In this scene McTeague tracks down Trina, who has lost two fingers because she is too miserly to consult a doctor. Now she realizes that her bags of gold will not save her from a vengeful husband.

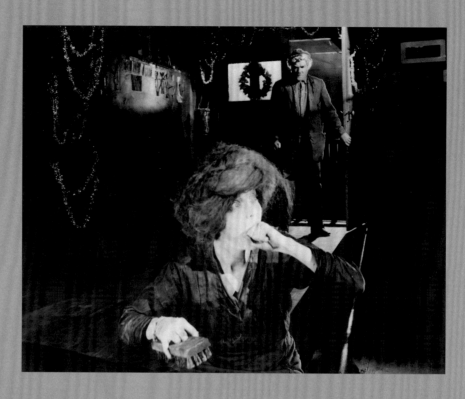

When Goldwyn was merged, Stroheim once again found himself under Thalberg's authority. "I soon realized that the change boded no good for me," recalled Stroheim, "as Thalberg and I had often crossed swords at Universal." The real problem was *Greed*. It ran seven hours. Contrary to what has been written about Thalberg's handling of the unique film, he weighed his options carefully. "We took no chances in cutting it," said Thalberg. "We took it around to different theaters in the suburbs, ran it at its enormous length, then took note of the places at which interest seemed to droop." When Joe Farnham and Howard Hawks cut *Greed* to two hours, many unflinching images hit the cutting-room floor. This shot of the murdered Trina was one of them.

Greed's climactic chase scene has McTeague confronted in Death Valley by his covetous enemy, Marcus (Jean Hersholt). "Every day, Gibson Gowland and myself would crawl across those miles of sunbaked salt," Hersholt recalled. "With real bloodlust in our hearts we fought and rolled and slugged each other. Stroheim yelled at us, 'Fight, fight! Try to hate each other as you hate me!'"

The first true M-G-M film, one that was planned and filmed on the Metro-Goldwyn lot and then released by Metro-Goldwyn-Mayer, was Victor Seastrom's *He Who Gets Slapped*. Mayer and Thalberg knew they were on their way when Marcus Loew booked the film into his newly acquired Capitol Theater for its fifth-anniversary gala. Norma Shearer and John Gilbert played young lovers in the film. "I wasn't too busy making my first picture for Leo the Lion to enjoy this dynamic young man with the flashing black eyes and sudden laughter," wrote Shearer. "He was a buoyant yet sensitive actor. He was able to combine fiery passion with tender romance." One of the high points of the film was a picnic love scene. "It was shot on a very hot day in a lovely orchard of feathery old trees," said Shearer. "I was lying on the ground next to a picnic basket, surrounded by daisies. Above me were the blue sky and Jack's laughing eyes. Suddenly the daisies and the sky and the laughter got beautifully mixed up and I felt my face covered with gentle kisses. Well, sometimes the loveliest scenes just happen."

With *He Who Gets Slapped* Thalberg created a critical and commercial success from an unsuccessful play, assisted by a brilliant director and "The Man of a Thousand Faces," Lon Chaney. "You should have heard," wrote the *Los Angeles Times*, "the spontaneous applause which greeted the preview of this picture at the Writers' Club, which is usually a blasé audience." In this scene, Chaney is flanked by Clyde Cook and Ford Sterling. *He Who Gets Slapped* was a box-office hit, bringing Metro-Goldwyn's first year to a promising conclusion.

Mexican-born Ramon Novarro became a star with his
sensitive portrayal of the Jewish prince Judah Ben-Hur.
Photograph by Arturo Bragaglia, Rome

1925

Marcus Loew hoped that the merger would provide him with more films. At the end of Metro-Goldwyn's first year, Louis B. Mayer and Irving Thalberg had not shipped the fifteen films required by their contract; they had shipped twenty-six. True, a number of these were made by Tiffany, Inspiration, and Buster Keaton, but all of them made a profit. Mayer still believed in providing clean, uplifting entertainment. "It has been my argument and my practice," he said, "that each picture should teach a lesson, should have a reason for existence." Loew could not have been more pleased. Thanks to the merger, quality films were drawing people to his theaters.

Mayer and Thalberg saw room for improvement. Other studios were pulling in more money. Why? They had stars. First National had the apple of Irving's eye, Constance Talmadge. Paramount had Gloria Swanson and Rudolph Valentino. United Artists had Mary Pickford, Charlie Chaplin, and Douglas Fairbanks. There were three ways that Mayer and Thalberg could catch up to the big boys. First, Thalberg could tailor vehicles to the talent he had, making stars of contract players such as Lon Chaney, John Gilbert, Norma Shearer, and Ramon Novarro. Second, Mayer could use lucrative contracts to lure the stars who were making films for the M-G-M releasing arm: Marion Davies, Mae Murray, and Buster Keaton. Third, Mayer and Thalberg could recruit new talent, bringing in established stars such as Lillian Gish

and unknowns such as Lucille LeSueur and Greta Garbo. By the end of 1925, Mayer and Thalberg had done all three. Their combined energy and ingenuity had wrought significant changes, not only in the company but also in the landscape of the film capital. New stars, blockbuster hits, and a profit of $4.7 million put Metro-Goldwyn ahead of every studio in town except Paramount.

"The Lasky forces at Paramount seem to be hanging over the fence gazing at Metro-Goldwyn in terrified awe," wrote Hollywood columnist Herbert Howe. "In fact, the Metro-Goldwyn lion has them all worried. They meander around their lots wishing they could borrow Novarro or Gilbert or Norma Shearer or Monta Bell or King Vidor. Bother that! They'd have to borrow Irving Thalberg to know what to do with them."

It was true that Thalberg's production methods had turned out profitable films. It was also true that his willingness to take a chance on unusual projects—*The Unholy Three*, *The Merry Widow*, *The Big Parade*, and *Ben-Hur*—had yielded sensational results. It was also obvious that long work hours and the stress of gambling with millions of dollars was taking a toll on the twenty-six-year-old executive with the bad heart. So was his unrequited love for Constance Talmadge. One night in late November when he was working late, editing *Ben-Hur*, he felt nauseated and faint. He had trouble breathing and was hit with a series of stabbing chest pains. He fell to the floor. Hospital doctors diagnosed a heart attack. The prognosis was only 50 percent positive. Mayer was terrified that he would lose a valuable partner and a cherished friend.

Almost miraculously, Thalberg began to pull through. The reason cited by his mother was the love of his work. He chose to recuperate in a sickroom that would allow for a movie projector. He wanted to continue editing the chariot-race sequence in *Ben-Hur*. "I'm beginning to think that Thalberg is a little Napoleon

after all," wrote Howe. "I suspect he has thought so all along, and there's nothing like faith in self."

Thalberg was unable to attend the triumphant premiere of *Ben-Hur*. "That glorious night found him sitting in a wheelchair," recalled Norma Shearer, the only new star who came to wish him well. "He was tired and pale, wishing he could see the sights, hear the applause and the shouts. His great moment was lost." Fortunately for Thalberg, there would be other great moments, and, as Shearer hoped, he would spend most of them with her.

Ben-Hur was a problem production inherited from the Goldwyn Company. After nearly a year of shooting in Italy, the film was nowhere near completed. Thalberg pulled the entire production back to Culver City, where he could supervise it. He and Mayer both felt that Francis X. Bushman's performance as Messala, the villainous Roman, was overshadowing that of the hero, Judah Ben-Hur, who was being played by Ramon Novarro. "My biggest, grandest scene was cut

out, the banquet with Carmel Myers," recalled Bushman. "Oh, that banquet scene, with those great columns! On this side a tiger and on that side a slave with a band around his neck, chained to these big pillars at the entrance. The most gorgeous scene that was ever photographed—cut out!" What remained was a short but effective sequence played outside the banquet hall, and Novarro's prominence in *Ben-Hur*.

The dehumanized life of the galley slave was graphically expressed by male nudity in *Ben-Hur*.

One third of *Ben-Hur* was shot in Italy, where female extras were not averse to appearing partially undraped. This version of the scene was only shown in Europe.

The chariot race in *Ben-Hur* was set in a place that did not exist. Art director Cedric Gibbons designed a circus maximus that would combine an outdoor stadium in a vacant lot at the intersection of Venice Boulevard and Brice Road (later La Cienega Boulevard) with a hanging miniature in which toga-clad puppets waved their arms. Eight hundred workers took four months to complete the full-size structure. On the morning of Saturday, October 3,

1925, the celebrated of Hollywood—stars such as Harold Lloyd, Douglas Fairbanks, and Mary Pickford—joined throngs of extras in the circus set. "Everyone in the picture business was there," recalled Norma Shearer. "There were forty-two cameras and thousands of extras and little cardboard dummies in the top rows in the distance fluttering their little paper hands as twelve chariots and forty-eight fine horses came thundering by."

The very first American photograph of Greta Garbo was taken on July 6, 1925, by New York photographer James Sileo on the deck of the Swedish liner *Drottningholm*.

In 1925, Irving Thalberg was barely twenty-six and already becoming a legend. "He is the one they call the 'Boy Wonder' of the movies," wrote *Los Angeles Times* columnist Harry Carr. The amazing ascendance of Metro-Goldwyn was generally credited to Thalberg, but at the end of the year, it was not his name that was formally added to the studio's hyphenate; it was Louis B. Mayer's.

Lucille LeSueur was one of the many performers Thalberg was grooming for stardom in 1925. In September of that year, she changed her name to Joan Crawford.

Norma Shearer became a star playing the drab secretary of a foxy lawyer in Hobart Henley's *His Secretary*. "I thought the story was vulgar," recalled Shearer. "I went to the little boss and made quite a scene, but he paid no attention. Not knowing what a plum role I had, I decided to play this stock character as a dried-up spinster, the first to arrive at the office and the last to leave. I decided not to wear any makeup, but to wear the prim smile of the self-appointed martyr. With this homely creature I discovered the balance between pathos and humor, and, after all my misgivings, the picture was a great success—which is the usual story." Edith Norma Shearer, whom D. W. Griffith had told to forget about movies, became Metro-Goldwyn's first female star.

In *Two Worlds*, a story by Adela Rogers St. Johns, Norma Shearer essayed a dual role. Florence (at left) is the well-bred graduate of a finishing school. Molly (at right) is a reform-school graduate. For over-the-shoulder shots, director Monta Bell used the newly arrived Lucille LeSueur, who was later known as Joan Crawford. "My first appearance before the moving camera was anonymous," wrote Crawford in 1959. "While Norma played the Tough Girl (full front, close-up), I played the Lady (with my back to the camera); when she did the Lady, I was the Tough Girl (with my back to the camera)." Shearer was smart enough to recognize Crawford's talent, raw though it may have been. "I found myself sitting in a car," she remembered, "and in the other corner was a girl with the most beautiful eyes. They were the biggest eyes I had ever seen. But they didn't trust me. I could see that. They never have."

Shearer excelled at playing dramatically different characters, even in the same film. She later wrote that she preferred the tough girl to the sheltered one. "I liked playing Molly best," wrote Shearer. "I decided to slick back my hair and wear a beauty spot and spit curls. I had a tight skirt, black silk stockings, and heels so high I could hardly walk. I tied a red tulle bow around my neck. With my hands on my hips and some chewing gum, I was all set up for business." Avoiding streetwalker clichés, Monta Bell worked patiently with Shearer to elicit two completely different characterizations. Although Harry Rapf changed the film's title to the misleading *Lady of the Night*, audiences responded to Bell's gentle humor and to Shearer's versatility.

Harry Earles, Victor MacLaglen, and Lon Chaney played a creepy trio in Tod Browning's *The Unholy Three*. "This bizarre and diabolical tale captivated Irving," recalled Shearer. "He saw in it the perfect Lon Chaney role, that of a ventriloquist who bosses a carnival strongman and a midget into dreadful crimes." While still at Universal, Thalberg had observed the creative affinity Chaney shared with Browning. It gave *The Unholy Three* a unique dimension, and the film grossed almost as much as *He Who Gets Slapped*. More importantly, it made Chaney Metro-Goldwyn's first male star. *The Unholy Three* had a further distinction. By teaming Chaney and Browning at M-G-M, Thalberg launched the American horror film.

The Masked Bride was Mae Murray's first film as a Metro-Goldwyn player. Head art director Cedric Gibbons, who designed this set, believed moving-picture settings should be more than just backdrops. "Make the sets act," he said. Making Murray act was another matter. "The future of Mae Murray as a screen star seems somewhat problematic," wrote Harry Carr. "She is artificial—avowedly and intentionally so. In a way it can be said that she doesn't act at all. She goes from one pose to another. But she comes the nearest to knowing what pictures are for and what they are all about of anyone who has ever tried to figure them out. That is to say she is purely pictorial. Other stars tell stories of imagined words. She tells stories in pictures."

With some misgivings, Thalberg assigned Erich von Stroheim to direct Mae Murray in a version of Franz Lehar's beloved 1905 operetta *The Merry Widow*. "Irving was not one to underestimate Mr. von Stroheim's extraordinary talent," recalled Shearer, "and so he brought his nemesis back." In this typically Stroheim scene, Danilo (John Gilbert) is seducing Sally O'Hara (Mae Murray) while accompanied by seminude, blindfolded violinists. One reviewer wrote: "Jack Gilbert has never appeared to better advantage. Where others might have invested scenes of promiscuous lovemaking with crudities, Gilbert suffuses them with the fire of irresponsible romance."

In *The Merry Widow*, Stroheim's propensity for decadence put John Gilbert into a chorus line at the Paris nightclub Maxim's.

How would the famous "Merry Widow Waltz," a showstopper for twenty years, translate to a silent film? Stroheim shot it so that every beat danced by Murray and Gilbert could be matched by the orchestra accompanying the film in the picture palace. In jaded New York, audiences stood and cheered the scene. The astounding success of *The Merry Widow* could not bridge the gulf between Stroheim and Thalberg. Before the film was even released, Stroheim had abrogated his M-G-M contract.

The film that truly made John Gilbert a star and put the renamed Metro-Goldwyn-Mayer on the map was *The Big Parade,* a film written in a stifling cross-country train compartment by Irving Thalberg, director King Vidor, and playwright Laurence Stallings. The men were so hot that they worked in their underwear, which was difficult for Stallings, who had lost a leg as a result of the war. He put his prosthesis on the wall of the compartment, and it swung down, kicking Vidor in the chin. "When I recovered from the blow, the evidence of the swaying leg was all too real," wrote Vidor. "I could never again say to myself that the horrors of war hadn't happened. I have often wondered if this blow didn't contribute much to the reality and later success of the film."

Mayer was against showing Gilbert as an amputee in the final scenes of *The Big Parade*. The shot of Gilbert returning to the French girl he loves (Renée Adorée) was made on a hill in Westwood. His fall in the dirt was as brutal as the rest of Stallings's script. "Mr. Stallings was a charmer," recalled Shearer, "with his masses of dusty brown hair going in every direction like an unruly little boy's, and his artificial leg, which did the same thing. In spite of the 'hardware,' as he called it, he was never still, but always pacing up and down with his cane, running his free hand through his hair while explaining an idea for a scene in a soft Southern drawl."

The first established Hollywood star signed by M-G-M was Lillian Gish, seen here with John Gilbert in King Vidor's *La Bohème*. "Metro-Goldwyn-Mayer welcomed me with great banners strung across the streets of Culver City," wrote Gish in 1969, "proclaiming that Lillian Gish was now an M-G-M star. Looking at them, I said a silent prayer that they would be equally warm in farewell." To entice D. W. Griffith's unique star, M-G-M offered a six-film, $800,000 contract that included approval of the story, director, costar, and cameraman. Gish wanted to play Juliet in her first M-G-M film, but more than half of American exhibitors said that they would not buy a film based on Shakespeare. Gish had very definite ideas about filmmaking. "We often found ourselves subjected to Lillian's will," recalled Vidor. She told Thalberg that the cameraman should change from orthochromatic film stock (which accounted for the heavy makeup of the period) to the new panchromatic. "We can't handle it in our laboratories," said Thalberg. "We know nothing about it." Gish insisted, so Thalberg gave in.

1926

In January 1926 Irving Thalberg rebounded from illness with the resilience of an athlete. In June of that year, Mordaunt Hall, the *New York Times* film critic, attended a party at Harry Rapf's beach house. Hall marveled at the saltwater swimming pool and at the profusion of big names—Samuel Goldwyn, Marion Davies, Buster Keaton, Joseph Schenck, Norma Talmadge. What really caught his eye was Constance Talmadge's escort, who was none other than Thalberg, "an old head on young shoulders, the young man of twenty-six who supervises many of the productions made by Metro-Goldwyn-Mayer."

Thalberg was back at work, personally producing fourteen films. This was fewer than the previous year, but he was really responsible for many more. M-G-M was no longer releasing for other companies (except Rex Ingram), so the studio was taking up the slack, producing thirty-seven films. Thalberg had to oversee them all. Marcus Loew rewarded him by raising his weekly salary to $4,000 (more than $85,000 in 2008 dollars), with a profit share of 20 percent (paid from the profits of Loew's itself), and a yearly guarantee of $400,000. Hollywood executives with this kind of income usually bought limousines, mansions, and yachts. Thalberg bought a few rental properties and then turned his money over to his parents, with whom he lived in a rented mansion at 503 Sunset Boulevard* in Beverly Hills. His mother tried to make him work shorter hours, but it was no use. Thalberg loved making movies.

"Entertainment is Irving's God," said writer Charles MacArthur. "He's satisfied to serve Him without billing, like a priest at an altar, or a rabbi under the Scrolls." Only in the occasional newspaper or magazine article was Thalberg credited; never on the screen. "This was Irving's modesty," wrote screenwriter Ben Hecht. "Although he worked on the plots of some forty movies a year, cast them, edited them, and guided them, scene by scene, to the cameras, he never put his name on the screen as a participant. There was no 'Thalberg Presents,' or 'Produced by Irving Thalberg,' or 'A Thalberg Production.' Thalberg's reticence as a moviemaker was an irritant to his fellow Pharaohs." For the time being, though, Thalberg saw no sign of envy, either at other studios or in his colleagues. The arc of his career was pulling M-G-M with it.

Ben-Hur and *The Big Parade* were playing "road shows," limited-release engagements in key cities. These were especially profitable because of the mammoth movie palaces in which they were exhibited. The 5,300-seat Capitol averaged $50,000 a week. The 1,500-seat Astor hosted *The Big Parade* for an unbelievable ninety-six weeks. This one film stabilized M-G-M and made John Gilbert a household name. The average M-G-M film, however, played only one week and had to recoup its $150,000 cost in that week. There were, of course, second-run theaters and foreign releases, but these constituted no more than a third of a film's revenue. That one week in the city was crucial. Thalberg was primarily making films for a middle-class urban audience. He was also making films for women. He told his staff that single women persuaded their dates to see the film that they wanted to see, and that married women took the family to see the film that they wanted to see. Hence, he cultivated women writers and made sure that M-G-M groomed women stars such as Norma Shearer. That Ramon Novarro, John Gilbert, and Lon Chaney became M-G-M's first stars was no accident; girls wanted to emulate Shearer, but they wanted to swoon over male stars. In 1926 these stars were joined by Lillian Gish and Marion Davies. In less than three years M-G-M had gained six, and Thalberg knew how to maintain them.

"Lillian Gish can't be a bad woman," he told the *New York Times*. "That would be impossible. So, in Nathaniel Hawthorne's *The Scarlet Letter*, which she will now make for our company, she is a good woman. She only gives herself from ignorance and love. However, John Gilbert (whose characterizations in *The Big Parade* and *The Merry Widow* speak for themselves) is expected to be a lover. It is a fact—proven by our preview screenings—that women go to matinees to see him as a lover." Thalberg warned that deviating from an established image was foolhardy. "I could mention examples of giving a star a part that was unsympathetic to that star's public," he said, "and the resultant failure of the picture."

M-G-M had few failures and quite a few blockbusters. One reason for this was Thalberg's system of preparing the script in story conferences, and another was his practice of treating each film to a sneak preview. After the preview, theater patrons were asked to fill out cards describing their feelings about the film. Thalberg used these—and his intuition—to reshoot certain scenes. After a second preview confirmed his choices, the improved film could be shipped. "The difference between something good and something bad is great," said Thalberg, "but the difference between something good and something superior is often very small." Reshooting a scene at a cost of $15,000 might turn a potential loss of $50,000 into a profit of $100,000. It was Thalberg's method. "Movies aren't made," he said. "They're *re*-made." Numerous films shot by Thalberg in 1926 would undergo this process—*The Temptress, The Devil's Circus, The Exquisite Sinner*. The only evidence of this cinematic surgery survives in still photographs of scenes that did not appear in the finished film. Discarded scenes were a small price to pay for a miracle. At the year's end, the studio showed a profit of $6.4 million. Less than three years after its founding, M-G-M had become the most successful studio in Hollywood.

In 1926 Irving Thalberg was spending less time with his drinking buddies (writer John Colton, actor John Gilbert, and actor Jack Conway) and more time with the ladies. Constance Talmadge continued to elude him. The notorious gold digger Peggy Hopkins Joyce toyed with him. Norma Shearer waited patiently for him. And Rosabelle Laemmle was rude to him. He began spending time with Shearer. "They just seem to be going about together all the time," gushed the *Los Angeles Times* social column. A cheeky journalist said to Shearer: "Tell me if and when you are going to marry Irving Thalberg." "Oh, never," replied Shearer. "I hope no one springs a question like that on poor Irving. I am not going to marry anyone for ever so long. I am going to work and make lots of money, and, maybe after I have marked time in another jolly ordinary little picture or two, I may rise to the distinction of playing, say, Jenny Lind or Juliet. But then I shall have to expect drastic criticism!"

Don't was the title of an Alf Goulding comedy featuring Sally O'Neil, Dorothy Seay, and John Patrick. This film was one of fourteen Thalberg personally produced in 1926. Its sizable loss was chalked up to inexperience (and a lack of stars).

Jack Pickford (above), the brother of America's Sweetheart, was brought to M-G-M to dress up a number of films but found himself upstaged by the fast-rising William Haines (below), who even mugged in still photos, shifting their context from narrative reference to personal showcase. This scene is from Jack Conway's *Brown of Harvard*, the film that made Haines a star.

In *The Waning Sex*, Thalberg cast Norma Shearer and Conrad Nagel (in their fifth film together) as competing lawyers. "This was my first opportunity," Shearer recalled, "to play the slick career girl who turns out to be a little too smart for her own good. When she wins a case, she almost loses a husband."

In *The Devil's Circus*, Shearer's third film of the year, she played an aerialist who is raped by a lion tamer. Recalled Shearer, "Irving was reaching all over the world for talent, and so this film was written and directed by Benjamin Christensen, a distinguished director from Denmark." Thalberg engaged Christensen after seeing *Häxan*, his unflinching history of witchcraft. There was much discussion as to whether or not the studio should include a rape scene in *The Devil's Circus*. At first Thalberg declined. "Norma would never allow herself to be raped, no matter what the circumstances," he said. "She looks much too well able to take care of herself." Christensen insisted, so Thalberg had him shoot the scene two ways: in one Shearer was nude but for a robe, which the rapist snatches from her; and in the other editing of close-ups and a dramatic fade-out suggested the attack. The latter was preferred by preview audiences. Though it was solemn and implausible, *The Devil's Circus* was a hit for Shearer and M-G-M.

Joan Crawford got a boost from Edmund Goulding in his film *Paris*. He cast her as an Apache dancer who is reformed by an American millionaire. One day Goulding ordered the nervous twenty-two-year-old actress to take off her shoes. "Now," he said in his rich British accent, "spread your feet. Take a good grip of the earth with your feet and your toes. Draw the strength of the earth right into you! Strength is there! Use it!"

Greta Garbo's first American film was Monta Bell's *The Torrent*, in which she played a Spanish girl who goes off to become an opera singer because her small-town sweetheart (Ricardo Cortez) will not marry her. Both cast and crew tried to stifle laughs when Garbo acted this scene. She was supposed to be singing a languid love song but the only one she knew in English was the bouncy show tune, "I Want to Be Happy." She crooned it slowly and sadly: "I want to be happy/But I won't be happy/'Til I make you happy, too." After a few torturous minutes, Bell yelled "Cut," and the set exploded with laughter.

"What was that picture you directed in which two lovers drift in a boat through willow branches?" According to King Vidor, the only thing people remembered about *Bardelys the Magnificent* was a shot of Eleanor Boardman and John Gilbert in a leafy corridor. The image was hastily improvised by Vidor and artfully executed by William Daniels. The film has been lost to nitrate decomposition. After the blockbuster hits of *The Big Parade, The Merry Widow*, and *La Bohème*, and the August 1926 death of Rudolph Valentino, John Gilbert was declared Hollywood's "Great Lover."

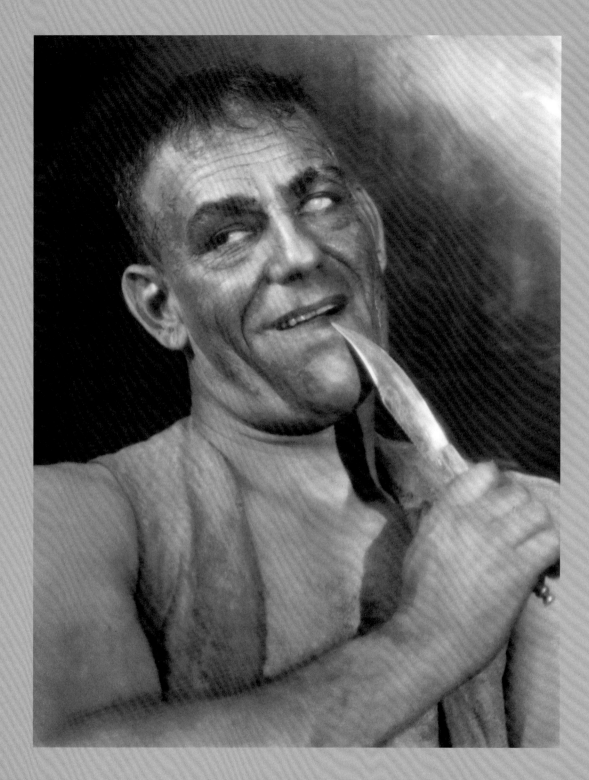

Thalberg's recruitment of New York journalists and playwrights introduced writer Herman Mankiewicz to director Tod Browning. The result was the weirdest Lon Chaney vehicle yet. *The Road to Mandalay* was the tale of a one-eyed saloon keeper who has raised his daughter in a convent without telling her he is her father. Most reviewers found the film off-putting. "The plot is so sordid and morbid," wrote *Motion Picture* magazine, "that were it not for the grip of the star's uncanny performance, it would in all likelihood be dismissed as a crass caricature of life." *The Road to Mandalay* was M-G-M's third-highest-grossing film of 1926. Photograph by Ruth Harriet Louise

After *La Bohème,* M-G-M's biggest moneymaker of 1926 was *The Scarlet Letter,* starring Lillian Gish and produced by Thalberg. "I lost my heart to him," she recalled. "He was a beautiful human being and a fine artist with wonderful taste." Gish suggested the novel to him at their first meeting. "Irving then asked me which director I would like. I suggested Victor Seastrom. It seemed to me that he had Mr. Griffith's sensitivity to atmosphere." With *The Scarlet Letter,* M-G-M had another film that played longer than a week. "For months *The Scarlet Letter* has been standing 'em out at the Central Theatre in New York," wrote a trade journalist. "It's still there. So are the crowds. Twice daily."

Irving Thalberg cast Garbo as a vamp in her second M-G-M film, *The Temptress*. It opened with a quote from the Indian writer Rabindranath Tagore: "Oh, Woman! Thou art not alone the creation of God, but of Man!" Audiences giggled at this title at the film's New York opening, but quieted down when Garbo appeared. Within a few weeks of its release, *The Temptress* was playing fourteen theaters in Los Angeles, an unheard-of number. It became one of the top-grossing films of the year, with nearly $1 million in receipts. Thalberg had another star. Photograph by Bert Longworth

Irving Thalberg and Norma Shearer were married on September 29, 1927. This photograph shows (from left) William Thalberg, Irving Thalberg, Henrietta Thalberg, Norma Shearer, and Edith Shearer. "There is a latent spiritual quality in Thalberg," wrote *Vanity Fair*'s celebrated Jim Tully.

"It even survived a business course in Brooklyn. Not strong physically, he gives one the impression of the poet. There is about his eyes a twinkle blended of mirth and sadness. His fingers are long, sensitive, and delicate—the fingers of a Richelieu—or a Machiavelli."

1927

Metro-Goldwyn-Mayer strode boldly into 1927, flush with triumph. The collaboration of Mayer and Thalberg had produced results beyond anyone's expectations. M-G-M could now boast the longest roster of stars in town, and the studio's 1926–1927 product sampler accordingly coined the phrase "More Stars than There Are in Heaven." The Culver City constellation included Marion Davies, Lillian Gish, Ramon Novarro, Mae Murray, John Gilbert, Buster Keaton, Lon Chaney, and Norma Shearer. To create vehicles for these lambent entities, Mayer authorized J. J. Cohn to build more stages and hire more employees. There were already more than a thousand people working within the gates of the studio.

Lawrence Weingarten joined M-G-M in early 1927 as an assistant to Harry Rapf, who was supervising both Shearer and Chaney vehicles. The young recruit soon saw how Thalberg's system worked. There was a distinctly hierarchical division of labor. "Thalberg directed the film on paper," recalled Weingarten in 1974, "and then the director directed the film on film." Weingarten also saw the pride that permeated the studio. "It was a big family," said Weingarten. "If we had a success, everybody—and I mean every cutter, every painter, every plasterer—was excited about it, was abuzz, was in a tizzy about the whole idea of picture making."

Mayer did much to promote the family image. He had the studio commissary feature chicken soup made from his late mother's recipe. He encouraged his stars to confide in him, but once in his office, they found themselves listening more than talking. Mayer was as grandiloquent as any stage veteran, and shamelessly manipulative. If he could not get his way by flattering or cajoling, he would resort to tears—or threats. These were not hollow threats, as both Erich von Stroheim and John Gilbert learned. "All women are whores," said Stroheim on one occasion. "My mother was a whore," said Gilbert on another. Both men were punched in the face and thrown out of Mayer's office—by Mayer. His dislikes were as violent as his affections, and his temper was hair-triggered. According to Conrad Nagel, who taught Mayer elocution, Thalberg coped with Mayer by taking a deep breath and saying, "Now, Louis . . ." (Mayer's friends and associates gave it the French pronunciation "Lou-ee.") "Now, Louis," continued Thalberg, "we can't afford to throw away talent because we don't like the personality that goes with it. Every new star means millions." Mayer would calm down and consider the business at hand.

Weingarten came to know Thalberg through weekly story conferences. Before long, he began socializing with him. Soon he was dating Thalberg's sister Sylvia, who was an M-G-M writer. Weingarten became a Thalberg intimate. "Irving had a sixth sense about a manuscript," said Weingarten. "He was a film doctor. You could go out [to a preview] with a film, and if there was something that didn't quite come off, he could put his finger on it. Some of the great films that came out of Metro were *re*made at his suggestion. He had that uncanny ability." Some careers were remade by him, too.

The fifty-nine-year-old vaudeville star Marie Dressler had fallen on hard times, so her friend Frances Marion tailored a script for her and hoped Thalberg would buy it. *The Callahans and the Murphys* had plenty of nose-thumbing and beer-swilling. "It's a cockeyed comedy," said Thalberg, "but I like it. Any special actress in mind?"

Marion suggested that the "great comedienne" Dressler might consider the role—if M-G-M offered her $2,000 a week. Thalberg gave Marion a stern look, and she knew he had seen through her. "Irving," she said, "Marie's a friend of mine. She needs a job."

"I thought so."

"She's a fine actress. I've seen her make an audience laugh one moment and cry the next."

"My theory," said Thalberg, "is that anybody who hits the bull's-eye once—it doesn't matter in what profession—has the brains and stamina to stage a comeback. So I figure that a woman who held the spotlight for so many years has been the victim of bad writing and probably bad advice." Thalberg's voice softened. "Send for Miss Dressler. We'll start the picture as soon as she gets here. Her salary will be $1,500 a week." The job put Dressler on the road to both solvency and stardom.

Greta Garbo was not as cooperative. She went on strike to avoid playing another vamp part. "Miss Garbo at first didn't like playing the exotic, the sophisticate, the woman of the world," recalled Shearer. "She used to complain: 'Mr. Thalberg, I am just a young gur-rl!' Irving tossed it off with a laugh. With those elegant pictures he was creating the Garbo image."

In addition to shepherding fifty-three films to the screen, Thalberg was dabbling in Hollywood politics. He helped Mayer and Conrad Nagel obtain a state charter for a motion-picture academy. "The motion-picture industry," said Nagel, "was the only industry where a bad product could make a profit. We had to do something." The Academy of Motion Picture Arts and Sciences was inaugurated on May 11, 1927. Thalberg was also in conference with Will Hays, the president of the Motion Picture Producers and Distributors Association (MPPDA). Hays was warning the studios that federal censorship was a possibility because of increasingly racy films. Something had to be done to placate both politicians and the public. In short order, Thalberg collaborated with E. H. Allen of Paramount and Sol Wurtzel of the Fox Film Corporation on a document entitled "The Don'ts and the Be Carefuls." This set of guidelines for evaluating both scenarios and finished films was adopted by the MPPDA in September 1927, and subsequently implemented by Colonel Jason S. Joy and the Studio Relations Committee (SRC).

On September 5, 1927, Marcus Loew died of heart disease at Pembroke, his Long Island mansion. He was fifty-seven. The soft-spoken multimillionaire was universally praised for his integrity and philanthropy. His death did not cause a shake-up at Loew's, Inc., since Nicholas Schenck had been running the organization for some time. Schenck acceded to the presidency without any fuss, and although business was a little slow (in part because of the sudden popularity of radio sets), he made no changes in Culver City. M-G-M carried on. The future looked bright, even when Paramount struck gold with a star named Clara Bow and moved back into first place. As Nagel said, virtually every movie was making money. No one was particularly upset when Mae Murray broke her contract and left the studio, or when Lillian Gish proved harder to cast than expected. Garbo and Gilbert were creating a furor. There was no need to worry.

No one worried on October 6, when Warner Bros. premiered *The Jazz Singer* in New York. It was the first feature film to use synchronized sound to convey the spoken word, but only in Al Jolson's musical numbers. When the film was premiered at the Criterion Theatre in Santa Monica on December 28, it was a different story. Film critic Edwin Schallert fumbled for words after seeing—and hearing—the film. "I am frank to confess," wrote Schallert, "that I have not known an experience to parallel it." The silent stars sitting in the theater had seen Jolson on the stage. In a stupefying flash, they saw a sound film capture his bigger-than-life appeal. They also sensed that sound could expose a less-than-dynamic talent. "The great game they had been playing for years was finally over," said Frances Goldwyn, Sam's wife. Thalberg was not so sure. He had seen the short musical films made under the Vitaphone

banner. "Novelty is always welcome," he told a reporter, "but talking pictures are just a passing fad."

Thalberg had other things on his mind on October 7. He was on his honeymoon, having married Norma Shearer nine days earlier. "Irving never knew he was being caught," said Mayer's secretary, Florence Browning. "After he was married, he said to me, 'Well, Florence, you never thought I'd get her, did you?'" The wedding was conducted in the Thalberg garden by Rabbi Edgar F. Magnin. Mayer was best man. Shearer's brother Douglas, a radio engineer, gave the bride away. Mr. and Mrs. Irving Thalberg spent a short honeymoon at the Del Monte Lodge in Monterey. The crash of the waves beneath the cypress trees muffled the first reports of a revolution.

Even before marriage made Norma Shearer the first lady of M-G-M, she looked on it as her domain. Here she shows where new "dark" stages will be built to replace the increasingly impractical glass stages. Many of these buildings are still in use at the Culver City facility, which was bought and renovated by the Sony Pictures Corporation in 1989.

In this scene from George Hill's *The Callahans and the Murphys*, Polly Moran and Marie Dressler play feuding Irish-American matrons who temporarily make up for a St. Patrick's Day picnic. At the Loew's American Theatre, a scene of Dressler and Moran pouring beer down the fronts of each others' dresses stopped the show—literally. "My mother never acted like that!" shouted an Irish-American patron. Light bulbs were hurled at the screen and stink bombs detonated. After the Ancient Order of Hibernians condemned the film as an insult to the Irish people, M-G-M withdrew it from circulation.

In 1927 Thalberg personally produced *Slide, Kelly, Slide*, which William Haines publicized by posing with Babe Ruth.

Mae Murray, here with Roy D'Arcy, sparkled as an M-G-M star for the last time in Dmitri Buchowetski's *Valencia*. Murray's new husband, Georgian prince David Mdivani, objected to Murray working in Hollywood but had no qualms about spending her salary. The admittedly "self-enchanted" actress began finding fault with Buchowetski. "You just don't like *any* director," Thalberg told her. When the film was a week from completion, Murray did the unthinkable. She surreptitiously left for Europe with her devious husband. "You must come back and fulfill your contract," Mayer cabled her. "Otherwise you will ruin your reputation." It soon became obvious that Mdivani was tossing M-G-M's cables into a Parisian wastebasket. Thalberg completed *Valencia* with a double, and, when Mayer cancelled Murray's contract, her career was effectively ended.

This photo of Gertrude Olmstead and Roy D'Arcy was made to publicize George Hill's *Buttons*. Modest comedies accounted for more than a third of M-G-M's grosses.

Three of the four films Hearst packaged for Marion Davies in 1927 were flops. Thalberg personally produced *The Red Mill*, but Davies still worried. "I went to the preview because I wanted to see the public's honest reaction," said Davies. "But where I thought I'd get laughs, I didn't. Nobody else cried at the drama, but I found myself in tears. I guess I was just sorry for myself. It laid a pancake."

When Clarence Brown's *Flesh and the Devil* was released in January 1927, the American public knew that Greta Garbo and John Gilbert had fallen madly in love on the set. Gilbert routinely played his favorite song, "Moonlight and Roses," for Garbo and gave her acting tips. "Every morning at nine o'clock he would slip into work opposite me," she said. "He was so nice that I felt better. I felt a little closer to this strange America."

Both on and off the set, Garbo and Gilbert were insepa-
rable. Fortunately, their ardor was photogenic. "I had
a real love affair going for me that you couldn't beat
any way you tried," recalled Brown in 1965. "In front
of the camera, their lovemaking was so intense that it
surpassed anything anyone had seen and made the
technical staff feel their mere presence an indiscretion.
Sometimes they did not even hear my 'Cut!' but went
on, to the cameraman's amusement."

Few M-G-M films were as unsettling as those directed by Tod Browning and starring Lon Chaney—and few made more money. Thalberg supervised Chaney's most profitable horror film, *London after Midnight*, in which "The Man of a Thousand Faces" played two characters, a steely detective and (here) a creature of the night. "The Man in the Beaver Hat" was created with makeup so punishing that it caused Chaney's eyes to tear and could only be worn for short periods of time. His dedication to his craft brought him a fanatical following and gave him a unique place in M-G-M's constellation of stars. After launching Chaney at Universal and teaming him with Browning at M-G-M, Thalberg could truly be called the father of the American horror film.

George Hill's *Tell It to the Marines* had Lon Chaney bereft of makeup and playing a Marine sergeant. It brought the biggest profit of 1927, so Thalberg had Frances Marion write her next story about General Pershing and the Mexican War. An avalanche of fan mail demanded that Chaney do another "scary" film. "I guess we'll have to turn him into a freak again," Thalberg said to Marion, and he cancelled her Pershing script.

When Greta Garbo refused the role of a kept woman in Edmund Goulding's *Diamond Handcuffs,* Thalberg replaced her with Pauline Starke (here)
and renamed the film *Women Love Diamonds*. It was not a success.

Thalberg changed the title of *Anna Karenina* to *Love* so that the marquee could read: "Garbo and Gilbert in *Love*." "Greta has a mysterious look," John Gilbert told Frances Marion. "It's half Occidental astuteness and half Oriental passion." The onscreen passion of an offscreen love affair created a cultural phenomenon. The film grossed $1.67 million, which made it M-G-M's highest-grossing silent film after *Ben-Hur* ($9.39 million), *The Big Parade* ($6.13 million), and *The Merry Widow* ($1.93 million).

In 1928, a European honeymoon and a string of hits gave Irving Thalberg the bloom of health. William Haines remembered him as "an extremely sensitive man. He was almost melancholy at times, but believe me, he could be tough. His strength came from his mother. She looked exactly like him. They both had those piercing eyes. Hers were demanding. His were more searching, almost without pupils. He had enormous intelligence, and a kind of animal mentality."

1928

Three months after the premiere of *The Jazz Singer*, everyone was talking about talking pictures; everyone but Irving Thalberg. When pressed for a comment on the "talkers," he was atypically laconic. "The talking motion picture has its place," he said, "as has color photography, but I do not believe that it will replace the silent drama any more than I believe color photography will replace entirely the present black and white."

Having spoken his peace, Thalberg gathered Norma Shearer to his side and departed for their long-postponed honeymoon trip. Their itinerary, prepared by Douglas Fairbanks, encompassed Gibraltar, Algiers, the French Riviera, Naples, Rome, Pompeii, Berlin, Heidelberg, Paris, and London. This was the first European jaunt for either of them. It was also their first chance to spend time together, away from M-G-M and away from Thalberg's family, with whom they were living in a comfortable but not entirely agreeable arrangement. Henrietta Thalberg ruled the roost, and she knew what was best for her son, be it diet or sleep; he was made to occupy a separate bedroom from his lovely young wife. Shearer tried to put a brave face on it. "Knowing that Irving was devoted to his father, mother, and sister," she said, "I thought it would make him happy to live with them until he got used to the idea of living with me. This hardly held the privacy that a bride and groom would desire, but after five months Irving and I were able to enjoy our delayed honeymoon."

One of the highlights of the trip was an appointment with the world-renowned cardiologist Dr. Franz Groedel, whose spa at Bad Nauheim, Germany, specialized in the hydrotherapeutic treatment of heart disease. Thalberg emerged from the waters feeling refreshed and energized. He and Shearer also visited Heidelberg, the setting of her recent film *The Student Prince in Old Heidelberg*. "I thought someone must have brought over part of the M-G-M back lot to make us homesick," laughed Shearer. "The real Heidelberg was just like it. They couldn't have done any better if they had gone to Culver City with the express purpose of copying our sets."

While Thalberg and Shearer were in Europe, he insisted on seeing no fewer than forty films, most of them at M-G-M's Paris office. These films included Jacques Feyder's *Therese Raquin*, Vsevolod Pudovkin's *Mother*, and Fritz Lang's *Spies*. Thalberg saw no sound films, which confirmed his indifference to them. He was in no hurry to end his three-month trip because of a little studio like Warner Bros. It was unlikely that Hollywood would embrace talking pictures while he was away. When he and Shearer were interviewed on their arrival in New York, she said: "Each country we saw has a distinct life of its own and a history that is great. But here we feel good to be back amongst our own kind, making a history that will be great also." They would soon be doing just that.

While the Thalbergs were abroad, the talking picture had gained a foothold, if not in fact, at least in corporate boardrooms. Western Electric and American Telephone and Telegraph owned sound patents. Warner Bros. had invested in the Vitaphone process, and William Fox in Movietone. These companies, counting on the insatiable curiosity of the public, joined forces and launched the sound revolution. The "First All-Talking Vitaphone Picture," *The Lights of New York*, was released in July. It was as popular as it was imperfect, and it started a mad dash to sound. Warners and Fox committed to wiring more than 1,000 theaters by the end of the year. Loew's only had 140 theaters to consider, but they were huge. In addition, M-G-M had contracts with 13,000 independent theaters. Meanwhile, Warners was grossing 500 percent more than it had the previous year.

Paramount began construction of "soundstages" at its Astoria, Queens, and Hollywood studios. Steel girders rose for a dozen others around town. Thalberg held emergency meetings in late May. For the first time in five years, he found Louis B. Mayer less than totally supportive. Mayer was distracted and preoccupied. While Thalberg had been busy making hits, Mayer had been cultivating the friendship of a politician named Herbert Hoover. Now Mayer was on his way to the Republican National Convention in Kansas City, Missouri. Thalberg got his attention long enough to secure the go-ahead for two soundstages.

Norma Shearer's brother Douglas was working at the studio in the special-effects department but had experimented with synchronized sound films. Thalberg appointed him the head of his own department, and then shipped him off to the Bell Laboratories for a crash course in sound. "Doug" was his own kind of genius, an inventor, and he took to the job. He found an unfinished film that could be enhanced by a sound track. W. S. Van Dyke had filmed *White Shadows in the South Seas* on location in Tahiti. Doug figured a way to add natural sounds and music to the exotic images. When the film premiered at Grauman's Chinese Theatre in July, the eminent director D. W. Griffith introduced Van Dyke, who had been his assistant on the legendary *Intolerance*. "*White Shadows in the South Seas* is a work of art," said Griffith, "and Woody Van Dyke is the artist who brought it into being."

Van Dyke could claim credit for the lyrical images on the screen but not for the succession of sounds emanating from the newly installed horns behind the screen. The most startling moment came at the beginning of the film, when Leo the Lion cut loose with three roars. Doug had recorded his roaring and then dubbed the sound onto the existing "Lion Head Logo." When *White Shadows in the South Seas* became M-G-M's second-biggest hit of 1928, it could honestly be called a "roaring success."

The newly dedicated Los Angeles City Hall served as a backdrop for this production still from the Lon Chaney film *While the City Sleeps*. Only M-G-M's two "part-talkies" (*Alias Jimmy Valentine* and *White Shadows*) were more profitable than Chaney's 1928 films. He was M-G-M's biggest draw, surpassing Shearer, Garbo, and Gilbert.

"As a creative producer, Irving Thalberg was a man of impeccable taste," wrote Lillian Gish in 1969, yet she left M-G-M in 1928 because Thalberg had failed to find a formula for her. She asked him to film a novel called *The Wind*, a grim parable of the hopeless fight to subdue nature. Victor Seastrom created a masterly film from it, but it was silent in a season of talkies. Gish became one of Thalberg's few failures, perhaps because she was too individual or perhaps because he was too involved with Norma Shearer's transition to sound. "I hardly think I will continue at Metro," Gish wrote the Moscow Art Theatre. "Theirs is such a large organization that I feel they haven't the room or the time for me." Fifty years later Gish's performance in *The Wind* was recognized as one of silent cinema's great achievements.

Another M-G-M film made on location in 1928 was *The Cameraman*, starring Buster Keaton, shown here with Josephine the monkey. Keaton's first film as an M-G-M contract star got off to a bad start in the story conferences. "Thalberg was in charge," recalled Keaton, "and he wanted—oh, I wasn't in enough trouble trying to manipulate a camera—he wanted me involved with gangsters, in trouble with this one and that one. *That* was my fight—to eliminate those extra things."

A gorilla named Bimbo (played by Fred Humes) chases Louise Lorraine in *Circus Rookies*, one in the series of profitable comedies starring Karl Dane and George K. Arthur.

"Marriage isn't a word. It's a sentence!" says John (James Murray) to Mary (Eleanor Boardman) in King Vidor's *The Crowd*. Showing a toilet in a feature film was unheard of in 1928, but this was the least of the innovations in Vidor's "Big Parade of Peace." The virtuosity—and sincerity—of this uncommercial project earned Thalberg an unex-pected profit. "It's the story of one of the crowd," said Vidor. "The protagonist does nothing unusual, nothing that everyone can't understand. Birth, youth, school, love, business struggles, married life, always against the background of the crowd—that is the motif."

Opposite: In William Nigh's *The Law of the Range,* Mother Lockheart (Bodil Rosing) loses one of her sons to a renegade attack on her covered wagon. M-G-M's westerns made money and served as a training ground for actors such as Joan Crawford.

In Victor Seastrom's *The Masks of the Devil,* John Gilbert played a Viennese aristocrat who is so respected that he poses for a painting of Saint Michael; in reality he is no angel. In this scene, he dallies with his best friend's wife (Alma Rubens). Seastrom used double exposures to show the satanic personality behind the dashing exterior, and Gilbert reveled in the flashy role. "It stamps Gilbert as one of the great dramatic actors of the screen," wrote the New York *Telegram. The Masks of the Devil* has been lost to nitrate deterioration.

W. S. Van Dyke had directed ten Tim McCoy westerns on location in three years, but filming *White Shadows in the South Seas* was his trial by fire. When the renowned documentarian Robert Flaherty failed to produce usable film in Tahiti, Van Dyke got the job. "I have been in the most squalid and miserable places under the worst pos-sible conditions," Van Dyke wrote from Papeete, "but never have I felt toward them as I feel toward this job and place. M-G-M has taken a few months of my life and put them on a hot griddle and watched them fry." This pho-tograph shows the wedding scene of Monte Blue and Raquel Torres.

William Randolph Hearst's production company, Cos-mopolitan, tested properties by publishing them in his weeklies. Joan Crawford read the serialized *Our Danc-ing Daughters* and then found out that Hearst planned to make it for M-G-M. "I stole the script, went to pro-ducer Hunt Stromberg, begged for it, and was given it," wrote Crawford. *Our Dancing Daughters* had a party scene that showed why Crawford had been winning Charleston contests for three years. "As Diana," wrote Crawford, "I was the flapper, wild on the surface, a girl who shakes her windblown bob and dances herself into a frenzy while the saxes shriek and the trombones wail, a girl drunk on her own youth and vitality."

"This much fun making a picture I'd never had," wrote Crawford. "We were a group of young moderns, and it was a way of life I knew." Here Diana (Crawford) is toasted by her father (Huntley Gordon), Norman (Nils Asther), and two sheiks. "*Our Dancing Daughters* opened at the Capitol in October to a $40,000 week-end, then to a big Monday matinee," recalled Crawford. "By nine thirty on Monday night, standees were five deep behind the last row with a solid crowd filling the lobby to the doors." When these figures reached Culver City, Thalberg told Mayer: "We've got ourselves another star."

Laugh, Clown, Laugh was Lon Chaney's most successful film of 1928. Thalberg supervised the adaptation of the David Belasco play about a seasoned performer's unrequited love for the orphan girl he has raised. Thanks to Thalberg's prudence and Chaney's charisma, the film was neither distasteful nor maudlin. Photograph by Ruth Harriet Louise

Opposite: *The Mysterious Lady* was the first Greta Garbo film to be shot entirely with panchromatic film by her favorite cameraman, William Daniels. The improvement was immediately apparent in the creamy rendering of her eyes, lips, and hair. In this film, Daniels created images that set new standards for photographic art. "Greta was so beautiful we could use any lighting for dramatic purposes," Daniels said in 1967. "On her films, my photography had more continuity. Using special lighting effects didn't handcuff the director. Her face was such that I could have shot in candlelight if the stock in those days had allowed it. But, of course, we used small lighting instruments to suggest that quality of light, and it was really quite effective for the times." After the work Thalberg devoted to a scenario, it was up to artists like Daniels to convey the story. "The director tells the story with shots," said Daniels. "The cinematographer tells the story with light."

"Irving was a motion-picture man utterly," wrote Lionel Barrymore, who in 1929 went from acting in Thalberg films to directing them. "He was also extremely young. I used to go into his office with the feeling that I was addressing a boy. In a moment, I would be the one who felt young and inexperienced. I would feel that he was not one but all the forty disciples. One day he knew nothing about the stage and about speech in the theater. The next day he knew all about it." This photograph of Irving Thalberg was made at the beach house he and Norma Shearer were renting from Ben Lyons and Bebe Daniels in the summer of 1929.

1929

Thalberg had avoided talking pictures for a year. In 1929 he made up for lost time. Two soundstages were ready, reinforced with concrete columns sunk twenty feet into the ground. Each stage had nine-ton soundproof doors and a concrete-reinforced sound-mixing room. Douglas Shearer had his new technology set and acoustical experts standing by. All that was needed was a project. Would it be a Broadway play by Donald Ogden Stewart or an original story by Frances Marion? Never one to do things by half measures, Irving Thalberg decreed that M-G-M's first all-talking picture would be an original musical. He liked the British director Edmund Goulding. This Renaissance man could write novels, songs, act, arrange hair, and direct—in fact, he could do anything but remember an idea he had had earlier in the day. Goulding told Thalberg a backstage story about two sisters in love with the same song-and-dance man. It was old, but that was fine. Everything else about the project would be new. Goulding wanted to call it *Whoopee*, but Florenz Ziegfeld had a prior claim on the title. A song provided the title for M-G-M's first talkie. A new team provided the song.

"I had the title 'Broadway Melody,'" recalled Arthur Freed, who was writing lyrics to Nacio Herb Brown's melodies. "And, funny thing, Irving said that since we, none of us, knew much about making a movie musical, we'd just experiment with this and not spend too much money." These were usually famous last words from the Boy Wonder, but this time he abided by them. *The Broadway Melody* had no stars, no far-off locations, no crowds of extras on huge sets. The only expense came when he wanted to reshoot "The Wedding of the Painted Doll" number. The scene had been shot from one angle, straight on. "That's not a motion picture," Thalberg said to supervisor Lawrence Weingarten. "It's a stage presentation!" He instructed director Harry Beaumont to reshoot, and he approved the use of "two-color" Technicolor. "This time arrange the cameras so we can get some different angles," said Thalberg. Doug suggested a way of saving money on the retakes. "We don't need the orchestra, Irving," said Doug. "We've got a perfectly good recording of the music. Why not just play the record and have the dancers go through the number? Then we can combine the film and the sound track in the lab." Thalberg approved the idea, initiating the practice of shooting musical numbers to a playback of prerecorded music.

The Broadway Melody was ready for release in February 1929. Thalberg's plan had been to open it at the Capitol, which was owned by the illustrious Samuel "Roxy" Rothapfel and managed by Major Edward Bowes. Playing this film one week at the Capitol would confirm M-G-M's dominance in the sound market. "It didn't play the Capitol, which would have sent it into regular release," recalled Weingarten. "It was road-shown at the Astor on a two-a-day basis. It was a fabulous hit. It won the Academy Award as the best picture of the year, which was a boost for everybody's spirits. *The Broadway Melody* proved we were still able to make great pictures, even in the new age of talkies." Thalberg's inexpensive experiment went on to gross $4.3 million, which put it on a level with *Ben-Hur* and *The Big Parade*.

In April, Thalberg made a very public retraction of his position on talkies. "Talking pictures are greater than any other medium of expression," he told the *Los Angeles Times*. "The novel, the stage, the silent screen are all representations of life. But this is not real life. In real life you take two years to court a girl and to marry her. . . . On the silent screen it was manifested with some photographic trick, such as dissolves of various scenes in the courtship. In the talking picture, however, it is played out just as it occurred—condensed, of course—with the people, the backgrounds, the words they spoke—everything. The talkie is absolutely the nearest thing to life, the greatest form of expression yet."

Having embraced the sound film, Thalberg began preparing his stars for it. "Some stars panicked, among them Lon Chaney and John Gilbert," wrote Joan Crawford. "I didn't panic. I didn't have enough sense." The studio hired voice coach Oliver Hinsdell, a Texas regional theater veteran. William Haines could not comprehend Hinsdell's references to "pear-shaped tones." Hinsdell accused Haines of being "lip lazy."

"I've had no complaints," replied Haines, who was described in studio gossip as a "catamite," an "invert," or a "fairy."

Greta Garbo refused to take lessons. "What do I need lessons for?" she asked huffily. "They know how my voice sounds, and I intend to talk English the way I do now." Thalberg deferred to her wishes. "Talking pictures will no more be the doom of the foreign player who finds difficulty in speaking English than it will be for the domestic player who has to master a dialect

and broad accent for a foreign characterization," he told the *Los Angeles Times*. "I am of the opinion that talking pictures will not interfere in any great measure with the success already obtained by foreign players in silent pictures." As he would soon learn, it was not the accent or even the timbre of the voice that would determine a star's future; it was the audience's expectation of how that voice should sound.

John Gilbert's first all-talking release was *His Glorious Night*. Hedda Hopper described what happened when he quietly entered the Capitol to see his film. "He settled down to enjoy himself," wrote Hopper. "The title appeared, and the credits, and then the picture started. Gilbert appeared on the screen with his leading lady and spoke the lines—'I love you, I love you, I love you'—whereupon the audience broke into howls of laughter! Jack never waited to see the rest. Chin tucked down in his collar, hat pulled over his eyes, he rushed out of the theater." This was not an isolated incident. In Los Angeles, a critic reported that Gilbert's audience "chose not to take his love scenes too seriously." In London, the *Film Spectator* critic described a cruel scene. "White-hot love speeches brought only snickers from the first-run audience at Loew's here. Snickers, too, which threatened more than once to become a gale of laughter. Quite obviously they were at a loss to know what had happened to their idol and most of them seemed a little ashamed of themselves for laughing. But they laughed, and all the talking pictures in the world, all the fine salary, all the publicity puffs, all the paid reviews, can never undo that laugh."

These events took place in late September and early October. By this time, every M-G-M star except Garbo and Chaney had made a successful transition to talkies. From all available evidence, Mayer used the studio's network of fan-magazine contacts to spawn a series of articles stating that Gilbert had a high-pitched voice.

No newspaper review had described his voice as high-pitched; most described it as sounding different from what the reviewer (and the audience) had expected. The myth of Gilbert's voice being high-pitched, even effeminate, was created by fan-magazine writers who were being secretly paid by the studio. If it seems odd that Mayer would set out to destroy an asset such as Gilbert (no matter how much he hated him), it should be mentioned that Gilbert's new contract (negotiated in late 1928) gave him $1 million for six films, at two a year. The contract had not been negotiated by Mayer or Thalberg; it had been negotiated by Nick Schenck, president of Loew's, Inc. Mayer expected that Gilbert would break the contract if enough abuse was heaped on him. In addition to having more articles printed about Gilbert, Mayer had the sound department equalize Gilbert's voice to make it sound thin. Gilbert was made to wait longer and longer between films, which also had inferior scripts.

That Mayer could wage this campaign without Thalberg's knowledge showed how far apart the two had grown. Mayer's infatuation with politics and Thalberg's absorption in filmmaking did not make for easy conversation at studio luncheons. M-G-M executives were increasingly referred to as either "a Mayer man" or "one of Irving's boys." By early 1929, Thalberg had grown so fed up with Mayer's absences and grandstanding that he spoke with J. Robert Rubin, the third member of the Mayer Group, about getting rid of him. Before Rubin could weigh in on the idea, the entire Mayer Group found itself under attack. William Fox had quietly offered Nick Schenck a huge commission if he could persuade Marcus Loew's widow to sell her controlling interest in M-G-M's parent company. All of Hollywood listened in disbelief in March 1929 when Fox announced that Loew's—and M-G-M—now belonged to him.

Faced with this shocking assault, Mayer, Thalberg, and Rubin closed ranks. Recent problems were forgotten as the three united against a common enemy. Thalberg would soon have reason to be grateful for Mayer's political connections. They stopped Fox's hostile takeover—and saved Thalberg from going to prison for income tax fraud. (He had been taking flagrantly improper deductions for several years.) The outcome of the thwarted coup was that the Culver City executives—Mayer, Thalberg, Rubin, and Eddie Mannix—were henceforth mistrustful of Nick Schenck and the New York officers. Yet even after they had formed a unified front, Mayer and Thalberg continued to drift apart. Had absolute power corrupted absolutely? M-G-M was the most prosperous company in America's sixth-largest industry. Mayer and Thalberg shared pride in its ascendance, and yet they were unable to share even the simple pleasure of the newly named "Sunday brunch." Thalberg could not stand Mayer's self-exaltation. Mayer was suspicious of Thalberg's self-containment. Neither man was willing to share the credit for an immense achievement. And each envied the other. "Irving wanted as much as L.B. was getting," said Mannix. "That touched off a rivalry between them. Irving was after the big money. And L.B. began to think of the day he would produce the pictures. It changed them both, and it never should have happened."

The last year of a decade always feels portentous and significant. This decade was called "The Roaring Twenties," "The Jazz Age," and "The Era of Wonderful Nonsense." When all was said and done, what did anyone remember about 1929? Everyone made money in the stock market. Talkies ended silent movies. Every nine-year-old was humming one of two songs: "If I Had a Talking Picture of You" (from Fox's *Sunny Side Up*) or "The Wedding of the Painted Doll" (from Thalberg's *Broadway Melody*). And the stock market crashed in October.

The Broadway Melody was M-G-M's first all-talking picture. "Sound equipment was being improved literally week by week," recalled the film's star Bessie Love. "*The Broadway Melody* sounded much better at the end of shooting than at the beginning, but Thalberg decided against any more reshooting because of the cost and time." This overhead production shot from *The Broadway Melody* looks odd. Where is the camera? There are no fewer than three cameras, but they are all concealed in soundproof booths, capturing different angles from static positions.

This is the angle seen by the center camera. Charles King is singing "The Broadway Melody" for a group of Tin Pan Alley musicians that includes, at far right, the film's composers, Arthur Freed and Nacio Herb Brown.

Although Thalberg attended the January open house of Will Hays's Studio Relations Committee (SRC) at 5504 Hollywood Boulevard (in the brand-new Louis B. Mayer Building), his 1929 films flouted the censorship guidelines he had coauthored two years earlier. *The Broadway Melody* dabbled in "nance humor," comedy involving effeminate characters. In this scene, Mary Doran, Charles King, and Eddie Kane are grimly tolerant of the "mad" costume designer played by Drew Demorest.

While playing football players and race-car drivers, William Haines (left) usually found an opportunity to ooze unisex appeal, usually to the chagrin of nearby actors—but not always, as shown by this still of him and Eddie Nugent from *The Duke Steps Out*.

Ralph Graves (left) played the "straight man" for some gay humor in a Ramon Novarro film called (without conscious irony) *The Flying Fleet*.

King Vidor's *Hallelujah!* was the first major film cast totally with African Americans. Vidor started shooting in Arkansas with silent equipment, but had to stop partway through and adapt to talkie technique. "Vidor has poured himself into this picture, designed as an epic of the Negro," wrote one reviewer. "He has packed in glamour and action and humanity. This picture is ammunition with which to meet those who say 'They never try anything new in the film industry.'" This posed publicity still shows *Hallelujah!*'s three principals (left to right), William E. Fountaine, Nina Mae McKinney, and Daniel Haynes. Vidor used improvised music to underscore images of life in the South. "I played the guitar and sang spirituals as far back as I can remember," said Vidor. "In my home town of Galveston you could hear the men on the docks, pushing cotton bales around and singing songs. I planned sequences where we would write the music out of the mood of the scene." In addition to using regional music in *Hallelujah!*, Thalberg had Irving Berlin write a catchy tune called "Swanee Shuffle" for McKinney to sing in a cabaret scene.

Marion Davies made her talking-picture debut with Lawrence Gray in the musical comedy *Marianne*. "Irving never lost his temper with me," said Davies. "He had plenty of reason to lose it, but he never did. He'd look at me and say, 'Why did you do that?' He could give you a stare that made you feel just *that* tall."

Even though he had a pronounced Mexican accent, Ramon Novarro (seen here with Dorothy Janis) effected a smooth transition to talking films. His first was *The Pagan*, a part-talkie that made use of his limited but well-trained singing voice. "The Pagan Love Song," written by Arthur Freed and Nacio Herb Brown, sold 1.6 million copies of sheet music.

Only two M-G-M stars were still making silent films in 1929, Greta Garbo and Lon Chaney. Audiences demanded Garbo films—even silent—so M-G-M released four that year. In this scene from *A Woman of Affairs*, Garbo studies a photo of Dorothy Sebastian. Thalberg had convinced Will Hays and the MPPDA to let him make this cleaned-up version of Michael Arlen's banned novel *The Green Hat*. Thalberg told Hays that the script was "practically a new story, taking all that is fine and worthwhile in the book, but building it on a new, clean foundation." However, he confided to associates: "Don't look for a Sunday-school proposition." In this scene, Garbo seduces John Gilbert on the eve of his marriage to Sebastian.

A Man's Man was a silent William Haines comedy in which his wife, Josephine Dunn, wants to become a movie star and meet Garbo. "Garbomania" was enough of a phenomenon in 1929 to motivate a film; in this case, a lost film.

In her second 1929 silent, Garbo played a San Francisco modern whose composure is unseated by the sweaty sensuality of Java. The film originated with a request Thalberg made of scenarist Willis Goldbeck: "Write me a story on the same lines of *Blind Husbands.*" Goldbeck took a John Colton treatment titled *Heat,* adapted it, and judiciously renamed it *Wild Orchids.* Theater marquees could never have countenanced "Greta Garbo in *Heat.*"

The third of Garbo's 1929 silents was *The Single Standard*, in which she enjoyed a South Seas idyll with Nils Asther.

The fourth (and last) of Garbo's 1929 silents was *The Kiss*. This behind-the-scenes photo shows Garbo and Conrad Nagel being directed by Jacques Feyder and photographed by William Daniels (above camera) in a Paris courtroom scene. Released in November 1929, *The Kiss* was proclaimed Garbo's last silent film, M-G-M's last silent film, and Hollywood's last silent film. A writer in *Motion Picture* magazine voiced this scandalous attitude: "In spite of unworthy stories, in spite of her stubborn silence in this talkie day, I would gladly pay for my own ticket to see a Garbo picture—which is the greatest compliment a reviewer can pay." Garbo felt the same way. "I remember that she saw *The Kiss* three different times," said her employee Gustaf Norin. "Once in Los Angeles, again in Pasadena, and a third time in Long Beach." She had to buy a ticket at each theater because she insisted on going in disguise. Photograph by Milton Brown

John Gilbert's fans were eager for his first sound vehicle. After doing a cameo in *The Hollywood Revue*, Gilbert made his talkie debut in Lionel Barrymore's *His Glorious Night*. Audiences laughed as he gave his all to some risibly overripe dialogue in this scene with Catherine Dale Owen. Critics were comparatively kind. "John Gilbert's voice is neither remarkable nor displeasing," wrote the *New York Review*. "It is simply not what one would associate with the Great Lover of the Screen."

Lon Chaney was worried that sound would destroy the illusions he worked so hard to create. He continued making silent films such as *West of Zanzibar*, an adaptation of Walter Huston's stage hit *Kongo*.

Opposite: Twenty-seven-year-old Norma Shearer played a convincing teenager in *Their Own Desire*. Ralph Winters was working on the film as assistant to film editor Harry Reynolds. "One day Thalberg decided to run the film when Harry was sick," wrote Winters. "I found myself in the projection room with Thalberg, Shearer, and a couple of other biggies. I was nervous as a cat. While we ran the picture, Thalberg gave me cutting notes. I was expecting the tough kind of treatment I got from Harry. Instead, every once in a while, Thalberg stopped the film and very considerately asked me if I was keeping up okay with his notes. What a doll that man was."

Ramon Novarro wanted to promote himself as a concert artist but felt that he would be better served by a photographer outside M-G-M. While filming *The Road to Romance* in Laguna Beach in 1927, he met the record-breaking flier Florence ("Pancho") Barnes, who knew a young Los Angeles photographer named George Hurrell. "I had George take pictures of me in the costumes that I used for the concerts I gave in my private theater," recalled Novarro. "Sometimes at M-G-M even when you would say, 'I don't want this picture to be published,'

you would see it published. I wanted to protect myself. So I had this set of pictures done by George. Every night I would take just one costume over (to his studio). And he took stunning pictures. I spent about a thousand dollars on them." Novarro's singing career did not go very far, but the photos convinced Thalberg to put plenty of songs in Novarro's talkie debut *Devil-May-Care*. The Hurrell photos (including this pose, made in January 1929) inspired Norma Shearer to commission some creative photography.

In 1926's *His Secretary*, Norma Shearer had transformed herself into a frump so effectively that when she went home in full makeup, she fooled her own mother. Seeing Hurrell's portraits of Novarro gave her a similar idea. Thalberg was planning to film the racy Ursula Parrott novel *Ex-Wife* but refused to consider Shearer for it; she was not sexy enough. "Norma planned her campaign carefully," said Thalberg. "She bought herself just about the goldest and most brocaded negligee she could find." Then Shearer went to Hurrell's studio. "I loved your photographs of Mr. Novarro," Shearer said. "Now there is a part in my husband's new picture that I must have. Can you turn me into a siren?" Hurrell's images persuaded Thalberg and his colleagues that Shearer could play the part. "We were all convinced," said Thalberg. "The results justified her instincts."

Even in hectic 1930, Irving Thalberg allowed himself the luxury of an occasional weekend trip. This one was to Coronado in a chartered Ford Tri-Motor with Athole Shearer Hawks, Virginia (Mrs. Jack) Conway, Paul Bern, Howard Hawks, and (above) Norma Shearer.

IV THALBERG'S M-G-M

1930

The first year of the new decade was hopeful for those who worked in the film industry, uncertain for those who were recovering from the stock-market crash, and both for Irving Thalberg. At various times during his childhood, doctors had stood outside his bedroom door and told his parents in hushed tones that he would not live to see thirty. Six months had passed since his thirtieth birthday. He had weathered the storms of corporate dissension, a hostile takeover, and Internal Revenue charges. He occasionally looked pale and tired, but for the most part he looked younger than thirty. He had passed the milestone but took not a single day for granted. He carried nitroglycerine tablets in his vest pocket in case of palpitations, and he occasionally remarked to Albert Lewin: "I'd settle for just ten more years." Events of the coming year would confirm that no matter how rich and powerful he had become, he could not insulate himself from the most basic elements of human existence: birth and death.

Thalberg was rich in 1930. Everyone who worked in motion pictures was. The talkies were playing to 90 million people a week. People who had never been to a nickelodeon were standing in line outside movie theaters. Warner Bros. was practically minting money; its 1929 profit was $14 million. Paramount was ahead of M-G-M again, but Nick Schenck was not worried. The Loew's theaters were turning people away. "They'll go see anything!" Schenck said. "We can make money showing blank film!" This was the mood on Broadway. Wall Street was more subdued. Economists were still assessing the damage done by the crash of October 1929, when 16,410,030 shares of stock had been dumped in one day, causing billions of dollars of both real and speculative wealth to evaporate overnight. Banks were beginning to close and, along with them, factories and shops. The term *depression* was being heard for the first time, and it had an ominous ring.

The most ominous sound in Hollywood was the voice of Will Hays. He was warning the studios that they had to regulate themselves or face government intervention. Local censor boards had been hamstrung by Vitaphone's sound-on-disk technology, but, now that every company was adopting Movietone's sound-on-film, censors were once again scissoring footage that they felt the public should not see. The "Don'ts and Be Carefuls" had proven of little help to Jason Joy and the Studio Relations Committee (SRC). Hays told the studios that if they could not come up with an enforceable policy, federal censorship was inevitable. This galvanized Thalberg, who stepped into the breach and offered to work with Joy to draft a document. There were conferences with Father Daniel Lord, a Jesuit educator who had helped C. B. DeMille film *The King of Kings*, and Catholic layperson Martin Quigley, who published the trade paper *Exhibitor's Her-*

ald. They proposed an industry code and drafted "Reasons Supporting the Code." Thalberg and Joy coauthored "The General Principles." Lord's overriding concern was that movies were creating "occasions of sin" that did not exist elsewhere. "We do not create these types of entertainment," countered Thalberg. "We merely present them. The motion picture does not present the audience with tastes and manners and views and morals; it reflects those they already have." Lord and Quigley went to work on a document that would address all these issues.

On February 17, Hollywood officially accepted the "Code to Govern the Making of Silent, Synchronized and Talking Motion Pictures." Producers were now required to submit both scripts and films to Joy and the SRC for approval under the new "Production Code." One of the first films to run the gauntlet was Thalberg's *Ex-Wife*. Other studios grumbled about favoritism when Joy approved the script with the proviso that Thalberg dump the title of the notorious novel and make no reference to it in the film's publicity. *Ex-Wife* became *The Divorcee*, but no one was fooled. As Norma Shearer tackled the controversial role with her usual energy, she had another consideration. "I discovered I was going to have a baby," recalled Shearer. "Such happy events were apt to creep up on one in those days. M-G-M had two pictures lined up for me. Would I be able to perform efficiently? How would I look in this precarious condition? Even if I could get away with it from the neck down, there are things that happen in one's face. Irving told me to keep my chin up and stomach in and enjoy the whole thing."

While Shearer glowed with a new kind of glamour, Thalberg dealt with his last two "silent" stars. Greta Garbo had finally agreed to a talking-film project. "If they want me to talk, I'll talk," she said. "I'd love to act in a talking picture when they are better, but the ones I have seen are awful. It's no fun to look at a shadow, and somewhere out of the theater a voice is coming." Cu-

riously enough, it was not Thalberg's story editor who found a project Garbo would approve; she found Eugene O'Neill's *Anna Christie* on her own. She felt that she could play a Swedish-American girl who is trying to put a stint as a prostitute behind her, but she thought the play was prejudiced. "She says it portrays Swedes as low characters," said her agent, Harry Edington.

"If she turns down this role," responded Thalberg, "I will stop her paycheck."

Garbo knew how important this film was to her career. For all the indifference she displayed, she did have a commitment to her craft. By the same token, Thalberg knew how valuable this insecure artist was to his company. He surrounded her with craftsmen she respected and liked: William Daniels, Clarence Brown, and Frances Marion. He cast the Broadway actor Charles Bickford as the film's romantic lead, even though Bickford carried a chip on his shoulder from the first day. Instead of being grateful for the most important project of 1930, Bickford complained about having to "play second fiddle to Garbo." Thalberg was as diplomatic as possible because the choleric Bickford was perfect for the part of the hotheaded Matt Burke. As Marthy, the waterfront drunk, Thalberg wanted to cast Marion's friend Marie Dressler. "But she's a Mack Sennett comic," protested Brown. Thalberg made a screen test of Dressler to prove his point; she passed it. The big question was whether or not Garbo would pass the sound test, and not merely on the set. Would audiences react to her voice as they had to John Gilbert's? Would it match the image she had created in ten silent films?

Mayer sat with Thalberg at the sneak preview in San Bernardino. There was a choked hush over the theater when Garbo appeared on the screen. After her first few sentences, there was a rustle of whispers, followed by rapt attention. "Garbo is holding them in the palm of her hand," Thalberg whispered to Mayer.

"La Garbo's accent is nicely edged with a Norse 'yah,'" wrote a critic in *Variety*, "but once the ear gets the pitch it's okay and the spectator is under the spell of her performance." The glib publication gave *Anna Christie* more than the usual nod. "Infinite care in developing each sequence, just the proper emphasis on characterizations, and a part that exactly fits Greta Garbo put *Anna Christie* so safely in the realm of superlatives that nothing less than a rave does justice to everyone concerned, including William Daniels, the cameraman." Despite freezing weather, the film's opening at the Capitol was mobbed, and it went on to become the year's highest-grossing film.

Lon Chaney was the last M-G-M star to make a talking debut. He was so anxious about the transition that he demanded a $75,000 bonus. Predictably, Mayer grew angry and refused. It was left to Thalberg to negotiate with "The Man of a Thousand Faces." Chaney was afraid he would lose too many of those faces to sound. "Lon Chaney once told me that speech made impossible about fifty of his best makeup devices," recalled Boris Karloff. Thalberg assured Chaney that he could use his voice to create illusions too. And he got him to agree to $50,000, which he would collect if his voice recorded properly during filming. For his sound debut, they agreed on a remake of *The Unholy Three*, but not with his usual collaborator Tod Browning, who was unavailable. Jack Conway guided Chaney through the film, which gave the actor five different voices to project. Chaney fell ill during filming but managed to complete the film on schedule and collect his bonus. *The Unholy Three* opened in July and immediately became a hit. Chaney's voice was as compelling, if not more so, than his pantomime.

As 1930 progressed, it appeared that Thalberg was favoring the studio's female talent. This was a response to the public's enthusiasm for Shearer, Crawford, Dressler, and Garbo. It also reflected Thalberg's fascination with the touring productions he saw at the Biltmore Theatre in Los Angeles. He was awed by Broadway luminaries such as Ina Claire, Katharine Cornell, and Lynn Fontanne. As the box-office appeal of his male stars began to wane, he bought stage hits for his female stars. "The play was a showcase for the woman star," recalled Lawrence Weingarten. "Mr. Thalberg believed that. That's how we built the female stars, the Garbos and Shearers and Crawfords." He was also looking for male talent. New players included Basil Rathbone, Robert Montgomery, and the Metropolitan Opera star Lawrence Tibbett.

Filming *Anna Christie*, Greta Garbo's talkie debut, made everyone nervous: (left to right) cameraman William Daniels, assistant director Charles Dorian, Garbo, and director Clarence Brown. In 1967 Daniels recalled Garbo's reaction to the first playback of her voice. She turned to sound engineer Gavin Burns and said: "My God, is that me?"

The most exciting male whom Thalberg greeted in 1930 was not an M-G-M player. On August 24 in Good Samaritan Hospital, Norma Shearer gave birth to Irving Thalberg Jr. The labor was a difficult one. "We had a mighty struggle," recalled Shearer, "before he decided to give in and face the world. It all starts with a smack on the bottom, doesn't it? He was upside down, stark naked, and looking rather unattractive. The first thing he was required to do was cry. It seemed to come naturally. After he'd made enough noise to let everyone know he was alive, he learned to smile. Irving was the happiest man in the world at that moment." Thalberg was greeted at the studio gates by a cheering crowd. He told them that his three-hour-old son had the intelligence of a three-week-old.

The bright reception was dimmed by sad news. A message had come from St. Vincent's Hospital. Lon Chaney was dying of bronchial cancer. Four days later, Thalberg was at Chaney's funeral, eulogizing him. "Lon Chaney was great not only because of his God-given talent," said Thalberg, "but also because he used that talent to illuminate certain dark corners of the human spirit. He showed the world the souls of those people who were born different than us."

The death of a colleague who was only forty-seven reminded Thalberg of his own uncertain health, but, as always, his associates saw him turn from introspection to the business at hand. Chaney's place had to be filled by a new talent, and Thalberg believed that Broadway would supply it. As 1930 ended, M-G-M was tallying a profit of $15 million. So far Hollywood appeared "depression-proof." Thalberg was justified, then, in luring Broadway stars with the promise of big contracts. He was eager to synthesize the best elements of stage and screen into a new type of entertainment.

A more relaxed actor in *Anna Christie* was Marie Dressler, whom Thalberg cast as the boozy wharf rat Marthy. "I loved doing that part," said Dressler, "because deep down, below the sordidness of her character, I wanted her fine soul to show through." Thalberg next worked with Frances Marion to create a film just for Dressler. Surprisingly, *Min and Bill* yielded two stars: sixty-two-year-old Dressler and forty-year-old Wallace Beery, who had been playing villains for years.

In 1930, three M-G-M films turned out so poorly that Thalberg gave up on them. "Why spend money trying to turn a lemon into a lime?" he asked rhetorically. The first film to be scrapped was a musical revue called *The March of Time*. The next was a Marion Davies vehicle called *Rosalie*; it was the second Davies vehicle to suffer this fate. In late 1928, *The Five O'Clock Girl* had been stopped in mid-production because William Randolph Hearst was displeased with it. This uncredited portrait of Davies was made in conjunction with *The Five O'Clock Girl*.

The third 1930 film never released was *Great Day*. It was shelved because Joan Crawford felt she was unconvincing as a naïve Southern girl.

Joan Crawford and Johnny Mack Brown went on location to Keene's Camp in the San Jacinto Mountains to make *Montana Moon*.

In *Our Blushing Brides*, Crawford played a fashion model. Her gowns were designed by Gilbert Adrian.

Thalberg sent the cast and crew of *The Sea Bat* to Mazatlán, Mexico. This photograph was made on February 27, 1930, by unit still photographer Bert Lynch.

In M-G-M's second year of sound, Thalberg had trouble finding properties for his male stars. Ramon Novarro liked singing opera in Charles Brabin's *Call of the Flesh*, but fans were perplexed by his arty leanings. Photograph by C. A. Pollock

In Fred Niblo's *Way Out West*, William Haines was cast as an effete city boy dropped into a hostile environment. The laughs were too often at his expense.

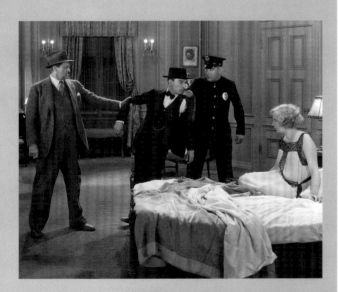

Thalberg wasted Buster Keaton's physical comedy in Edward Sedgwick's *Free and Easy*, in which Keaton plays a disaster-prone boob named Elmer Butts. In this scene, a studio cop (Edgar Dearing) removes him from a movie set where Lionel Barrymore is directing Gwen Lee and John Miljan (left). Keaton was able to improvise a few sequences, and the film was a success, but Thalberg's insistence on an immutable script would eventually break Keaton's spirit.

The first of the M-G-M silent stars to lose money was John Gilbert. His second talking release, Fred Niblo's *Redemption*, proved that his voice was not high-pitched; thanks to a series of journalistic hatchet jobs, no one bothered to find out.

In spite of the public's growing resistance to musicals and Thalberg's lack of sympathy for the idiom, *Good News* did well. Credit was due primarily to dance director Sammy Lee's staging of "The Varsity Drag," and eleven other songs by DeSylva, Brown, and Henderson.

Elliott Nugent shoots Henry Armetta in the face with his unfinished invention (a shaving cream applier) as Louis Mann and Robert Montgomery look on in Sam Wood's *The Sins of the Fathers*. Thalberg imported Nugent and his father, J. C. Nugent, from Broadway to write this heartwarming story.

"A moment! A madness! And she became . . . a DIVOR-CEE!" So read the advertising copy for Irving and Norma's big gamble. After her vigorous campaign to win the role of Jerry in Robert Z. Leonard's *The Divorcee*, Norma Shearer surprised the skeptics with her portrayal of a working woman who emancipates herself from a double-standard husband. "I haven't a doubt that there are hundreds of actual cases like this," Shearer told an interviewer. "The story has a feel of reality." Shearer's work in the film won her the Academy Award for Best Actress of 1930. On-set portrait by Milton Brown

Lon Chaney was the last M-G-M star to make the transition to sound. The public accepted Chaney's voice as readily as they had Garbo's, yet Chaney was unable to savor his triumph. Photograph by George Hurrell

Opposite: *The Big House* was Thalberg's most stark, unsentimental film since *The Big Parade*. In this scene, Chester Morris is led down the stairs to solitary confinement; apparently the still photographer thought that Morris coming up the stairs would make a better shot. *The Big House* was M-G-M's fourth most profitable film of 1930.

George Hurrell was brought to M-G-M in January 1930 to maintain Shearer's new image, but the star who benefited most from his work was Joan Crawford, seen here in a pose from one of the many sittings she enjoyed with the artist that year.

Greta Garbo's stardom owed a great deal to cameraman William Daniels and portrait photographer Clarence Bull. Each artist used light and shadow to etch Garbo's image in the public consciousness. Photograph by Clarence Bull

A publicity department collage shows M-G-M's 1931 star power. From top left: Greta Garbo, Marion Davies, Norma Shearer, Joan Crawford; second row, Robert Montgomery, Marie Dressler, John Gilbert, Ramon Novarro; third row, Alfred Lunt, Lynn Fontanne, Wallace Beery, Lawrence Tibbett; bottom row, William Haines, Buster Keaton, and Jackie Cooper.

1931

For the first time since the founding of M-G-M, Thalberg visibly reduced his workload. The studio had released fifty films in 1930. Of these, Thalberg had personally supervised a dozen. More than sixty releases were planned for 1931. Thalberg would be officially supervising only two: a Greta Garbo film called *Inspiration* and a Norma Shearer film based on Noël Coward's play *Private Lives*. In actuality his workload was no lighter. He may have had only two films to shepherd personally, but he still had to oversee sixty. As vice president in charge of production, he was truly in charge. Keeping tabs on each film from the purchase of a literary property to its last preview, Thalberg put his imprint on it. Every M-G-M film, no matter who else worked on it, was made by him.

Yet neither the studio nor its films bore Thalberg's name. "If you can give yourself credit," said Thalberg, "you don't need to put it there." Whether this attitude was the result of logic, indifference, modesty—or all three—was immaterial. The public saw the face of Louis B. Mayer astride the studio, as prominent and formidable as the leonine logo. The assumption that he played an active part in the filmmaking process was widespread and fanciful. As Eddie Mannix, his other vice president, later said, "Mayer began to believe that he could make films as well as Thalberg." And why not? Mayer had just gotten Herbert Hoover elected to the presidency of the United States (in part by bankrolling the Republican convention). If he could do that while managing the biggest movie studio in the world, why couldn't he make the films themselves? Why not? Because he did not have what Thalberg had. Few of Thalberg's associates had it. If they did, they did not have it to the same degree. Genius can be defined as the ability to make something from nothing. Thalberg had genius.

Many of Mayer's colleagues would later say that he had a genius for management. That was obvious. He did not have a faculty for filmmaking, and his taste was lamentably middlebrow. "To sell Mayer a script," said publicity director Howard Strickling, "all you needed was a story of mother love and a sentimental theme played on violins." He never read books. He refused to read scripts. He relied on Kate Corbaley, a story-department reader nicknamed Scheherazade, to synopsize submissions and read them to him in vibrant, breathless orations. By comparison, Thalberg was an avid reader. "He had a fanatic fondness for good writing," wrote playwright Bayard Veiller. "He even liked to read books for his own amusement. Picture people do not. They read books looking for material to put on the screen. But Thalberg read all kinds—books on science, books on religion." He read Epictetus, Homer, Hegel, Kant, Schopenhauer, Freud, Jung, and Krafft-Ebing. Had he confined himself to the Katzenjammer Kids, it would have made no difference. He understood drama and could apply that understanding in a story conference. The writers assembled at those conferences comprised, as *Fortune* magazine put it, "more members of the literati than it took to produce the King James Version of the Bible." To round out his writing staff, Thalberg had engaged literary lights such as F. Scott Fitzgerald, Anita Loos, Dorothy Parker, P. G. Wodehouse, Sidney Howard, William Faulkner, S. N. Behrman, George Kelly, James M. Cain, Robert Benchley, Donald Ogden Stewart, and George S. Kaufman. Mayer, who never attended story conferences, contributed little to the day-to-day process of making films.

During the transition from silent films to sound, Mayer was absent from the studio more days than he was present. As a result, Thalberg had to renew contracts that dated from the merger and were expiring. Shearer signed a three-picture contract for $100,000. William Haines's new contract cut his salary from $1,750 a week to $1,500. Like Ramon Novarro, Haines was slipping, so he had no choice but to accept the cut. When Mayer was present, Thalberg would sometimes help him with difficult stars. Novarro recalled a meeting in which Mayer tried to rush him to sign a contract because he (Mayer) was leaving on a trip. While Mayer hurried Novarro, Thalberg distracted him by jingling his keys and bouncing coins off a glass desktop. Novarro saw through the game and angrily left the meeting. After Mayer departed, Thalberg reached an agreement with Novarro.

While Mayer was away, Thalberg groomed the thirty-year-old stage actor Clark Gable, reworking his appearance, having the publicity department emphasize his enjoyment of riding and hunting, and putting him in nine consecutive films. When Mayer returned, Gable was on the verge of stardom. He was also involved in an adulterous romance with Joan Crawford. Mayer called Gable to his office and told him to choose between Crawford and stardom. "He would have ended my career in fifteen minutes," recalled Gable. "And I

had no interest in becoming a waiter." After resolving the crisis, Mayer confronted Thalberg, demanding to know why these things had happened.

"If you were ever here, L.B., you'd know why," replied Thalberg, referring to Mayer's political trips.

"Wherever I am, Irving, I am the head of this studio."

"Don't I know it?" snapped Thalberg. "Isn't that why Schenck pays you a million dollars a year?"

Thalberg's set-to with Mayer highlighted two sensitive issues. The partners had established a unique, intense bond on Mission Road. As much as anything else, it accounted for the extraordinary ascendance of M-G-M. After five years, the warm concord had cooled into a chilly civility. Mayer and Thalberg seemed unable to speak the same language. Thalberg was painfully aware of his alienation yet could not bridge the gap. He further distanced himself from Mayer by repeated demands for salary increases. In several instances Mayer had to sacrifice points from his own profit percentage. In 1929 Mayer had reduced his share from 53 percent to 43 percent so that Thalberg's could jump from 20 percent to 30 percent. In 1932 he would sacrifice points so that Thalberg could have 37.5 percent. "The boy is money mad," Mayer grumbled. His daughter Irene disagreed. "I found Irving's demands understandable," she wrote. "No one else was a saint about money; there was no reason for him to be. He had a growing family, his life span was limited, but, above all, his value was incalculable."

Another of Thalberg's concerns was Norma Shearer's career. The talkies had rearranged the hierarchy of Hollywood, displacing perennials like Mary Pickford, John Gilbert, and Gloria Swanson. Popularity polls conducted by the exhibitors' magazines *Motion Picture Herald* and *Film Daily* consistently showed Marie Dressler, Will Rogers, Janet Gaynor, Greta Garbo, and Charles Farrell in the top five spots, followed by Shearer and Crawford. (Only M-G-M and the Fox Film Corporation had the top stars of this period.) To Thalberg, his wife's status was all-important. He would keep her in the top ten for most of her fifteen years of stardom, even during year-long absences. He accomplished this by putting her in roles that both anticipated trends and responded to the fantasies of her fans. In 1931, female moviegoers wanted to see sexually adventurous heroines on the screen, and Thalberg was willing to oblige them. The properties he chose—*Private Lives*, *The Guardsman*, and *Strange Interlude*—betokened Thalberg's newfound fascination with the theater.

Broadway in the 1930s boasted an enviable array of stars: Ethel Barrymore, Alfred Lunt and Lynn Fontanne, Helen Hayes, Katharine Cornell, and Ina Claire. To Thalberg, these luminaries, not movie stars, personified the height of dramatic art and the apex of glamour. His fervent wish was to capture the magic of a Broadway performance on film. He had seen this in Al Jolson's thrilling film appearances. He had also seen Broadway hits fall flat when performed by Hollywood stars. He reasoned that having stage stars repeat their performances in cinematically fluid versions of their plays would synthesize theater and film into a new art form. He approached every star on Broadway, but only Helen Hayes and the Lunts accepted his invitation. "Thalberg was, in his way, a clever man," recalled Lynn Fontanne. "He had taste and intelligence, and he seriously wanted to make good movies."

Lunt and Fontanne in *The Guardsman* became what Mayer would condescendingly describe as a "prestige picture." It got outstanding reviews, played to packed houses at the Astor for ten weeks and even moved to the Capitol, but it failed to engage a nationwide audience. Its prestige lay in the perception that M-G-M (and not Paramount or Warner Bros.) could lure the Lunts to Hollywood. But Thalberg could not keep them there. "He wanted slaves, not actors," said Fontanne, "and we'd worked too hard for our independence." Thalberg was taken aback by Fontanne's candor. "Your wife will get all my stage roles," she said to

his face, "and I'll get the B pictures." There were no B pictures at M-G-M, but when Thalberg filmed Fontanne's Broadway hit *Strange Interlude*, Shearer starred in it.

For all the work and care Thalberg put into theatrically derived films, his biggest hits of 1931 were *Trader Horn* (a jungle epic), *Mata Hari* (a Garbo vehicle), two Marie Dressler comedies cowritten by his sister, and *Possessed*, the torrid teaming of Crawford and Gable. America was in the grips of a depression. Six million workers were unemployed. In two years, movie attendance had dropped from the all-time high of 90 million a week to 60 million. Paramount had seen its profits plunge from $12 million to $6 million, and was so panicked that it was selling its theaters to Fox. Warner Bros., after soaring to the top with talkies, ended 1931 with a loss of $7 million. M-G-M ended the year with a profit of $12 million. Mayer and Thalberg were not working together as well as they had, but they were still working together.

"Louis B. Mayer was one of the great producers," recalled Ben Hecht, who was an award-winning playwright before he came to Hollywood and became, arguably, its greatest screenwriter. "Mayer was in the business to make money, and he did it by diverting the largest number of people, not by pleasing the brightest." In 1931 Hecht was doing uncredited rewrites on Thalberg movies that his partner Charles MacArthur was writing. "But Thalberg was the genius," said Hecht. "I worked with Irving, and he was different. Irving was a natural-born storyteller. He had a flair for telling movie stories, and he knew about the medium—more than most writers knew. He was like a man who hadn't learned to write, who hadn't even learned to think, because he hadn't the faintest idea what was going on anywhere in the world except in his office. He lived two thirds of his time in the projection room. He saw only movies. He never saw life. He had never noticed life. He was a hermit. He hadn't the faintest idea what human beings did—but he knew what their shadows should do."

After King Vidor directed Wallace Beery and Jackie Cooper in *The Champ*, Thalberg asked him: "How did you ever learn to be so human?" Vidor liked to stand outside Grauman's Chinese Theatre when *The Champ* was letting out. "I would watch the people come out with their handkerchiefs in their hands, wiping their eyes." Beery was yet another actor lifted from supporting roles to stardom by a Thalberg hunch.

Polly Moran has just been locked in a steam room by Marie Dressler in this scene from *Reducing*. The Moran-Dressler comedies, poking fun at small-town mores and family hierarchy, brought Metro a profit of $1.2 million in 1931.

After making *Parlor, Bedroom, and Bath*, Buster Keaton filmed both French-language and German-language versions for Thalberg. Keaton is seen here with Leni Stengel in *Casanova wider Willen*, the German version; in the background is Keaton's Beverly Hills mansion, the setting for all three versions.

Thalberg cast John Gilbert in *West of Broadway*, a poor film with which Louis B. Mayer hoped to break Gilbert's contract. With a better film, Gilbert could have made an outstanding cowboy, but *West of Broadway* was a millstone for the struggling star. "People—just people—put the stamp of disapproval on Jack Gilbert's voice," recalled Norma Shearer. "They thought it didn't match his personality. Was this true? I remember it being vibrant, alive—like he was. It is true that his onscreen diction was overly precise and made him sound pedantic at times, but this could have been overcome. But when the fan magazines wrote that he was doomed, Jack began to believe that he was. The fear of failure robbed him of the most necessary thing for an actor—his ego. Without it, he was lost."

Almost a year after Greta Garbo had made *Anna Christie*, she remade the film in German, securing Thalberg's permission to make the film more naturalistic than its predecessor.

Opposite: Bringing Broadway to Hollywood was the key to Thalberg's new concept of cinema. The first stage star to accept his invitation was Helen Hayes, and her first film was *The Sin of Madelon Claudet*, the story of a French girl who falls in love with an American artist (Neil Hamilton).

The most profitable M-G-M film of 1931 was shot in the wilds of Africa. Or was it? Mutia Oomooloo, Duncan Renaldo, Edwina Booth, and Harry Carey spent as much time shooting scenes for *Trader Horn* in Culver City as they had in Africa; this photograph, however, was made in Africa.

Opposite: The second Broadway luminary to answer Thalberg's call was not one star but a team: the celebrated acting couple, the Lunts. In *The Guardsman*, Alfred Lunt and Lynn Fontanne portrayed married stage stars (like themselves) who perform Maxwell Anderson's *Elizabeth the Queen*.

In later years, Thalberg would be criticized for casting Caucasians as Asians, but in 1931 he used authentic Native Americans in his films. White Spear, a Cherokee Indian, portrayed a murderous Mohican in *The Great Meadow*. "Members of my race make good actors, for they are natural in every gesture and movement," said the college-educated White Spear. "When we go on location to a reservation, it is up to me to get the sanction of the old chiefs. The older men consent grudgingly sometimes, for they are of the old school, but I have yet to fail in securing their cooperation." *The Great Meadow* did not hurt the Native American image, but its meandering plot made it a flop.

Opposite: *The Easiest Way* was Thalberg's contribution to the controversial "kept woman" cycle, flouting the Production Code he had coauthored. This scene with Constance Bennett and Robert Montgomery was made on location at Yosemite National Park.

Bachelor Father was one of three charming (but unsuccessful)
Marion Davies films released in 1931. Portrait by James Manatt

In *Strangers May Kiss*, Norma Shearer played a modern woman who believes that she, like a man, "can love, and ride on." In this scene, Lisbeth sits alone on Christmas Eve in New York. Her journalist lover Alan (Neil Hamilton) shows up unexpectedly and invites her to live with him in Mexico. Lisbeth has to test her philosophy sooner than she expects when Alan dumps her in a remote village so he can go unencumbered to his next assignment. Instead of crumbling with self-pity, Lisbeth bravely picks herself up and rides on. Shearer's portrayal of a woman gathering her strength elicited spontaneous applause from the premiere audience at the Carthay Circle Theatre.

Pauline Frederick played Joan Crawford's wayward mother in *This Modern Age*. Crawford had idolized Frederick for years and was thrilled to be working with her. "If they'll give this child a chance," said Frederick, "she'll do big things. Joan is an actress." Thalberg agreed and gave Crawford challenging parts.

Lionel Barrymore played Norma Shearer's errant father in *A Free Soul*, Adela Rogers St. Johns's story of an iconoclastic girl. "*A Free Soul* was in part the true story of Adela's upbringing by her father Earl Rogers," recalled Shearer. "Having lost his wife, and wanting a son, this criminal lawyer brought Adela up according to a man's standards, taking her with him to bars to celebrate his latest courtroom triumph. The worldly little girl learned to sleep on the bar while her father sought the elusive comfort of drink." Photograph by Milton Brown

In *A Free Soul*, Shearer and Gable glowed with sexual energy. "There were several roles I wanted very badly," recalled Joan Crawford. "One was *A Free Soul*. I was dying to do it. And Adela wanted me to. But Norma got it anyway." In 1931 she usually did. "Norma was the queen," said George Hurrell, "and what she wanted, she got." Photograph by Milton Brown

Shearer may have gotten *A Free Soul,* but Crawford got Gable as her leading man in three films that year. The chemistry between Crawford and Gable in *Possessed* nearly caused a scandal. "Clark Gable's love scenes broke up his first marriage," wrote Buster Keaton. "Like all of us, he was on the spot: look like you're enjoying it and your wife jumps to conclusions. Look like you're not and you're out of a job." Photograph by Milton Brown

When Sam Manatt made this shot on the set of *Possessed*, Gable was so popular that even his silhouette was recognizable. Yet, he was insecure because Thalberg had cast him as an affluent attorney. "Will people accept me as this Harvard guy?" he asked writer Lenore Coffee.

East Los Angeles stood in for Erie, Pennsylvania, in this scene from *Possessed*. In this production still, Clarence Brown directs Joan Crawford and Wallace Ford. Crawford was not M-G-M's biggest star, but by the end of the year she had brought the company $985,000 in profits (compared to Shearer's $813,000) and been cast in the most important film of the coming year, *Grand Hotel*.

133

Greta Garbo performed the medium and close angles of the exotic dance to the Lord Shiva in *Mata Hari*. Broadway dancer June Knight doubled the long shots. The scene created a sensation. When *Mata Hari* was reissued eight years later, the Production Code Administration censored the striptease part of the dance and M-G-M threw away the trims. A complete print of the film is in the collection of the Brussels Cinémathèque Royale.

Opposite: Greta Garbo was M-G-M's star supreme in 1931, bringing $1.6 million in profits. She was the only major star of silent films who became a bigger star in sound films. Photograph by Milton Brown

At thirty-three, Irving Thalberg wielded the power of a renaissance prince and earned a princely compensation. He carried both with a studied reserve. Writer Anita Loos was unimpressed. "Irving was still a rather pathetic figure," wrote Loos. "His natural pallor was intensified by long hours in offices and projection rooms, shut away from the California sunshine. I was enormously touched that the shoulders of Irving's jacket were too obviously padded, in order to make him seem more grown-up and robust." On

July 15, 1932, Thalberg was photographed with his wife and Sid Grauman at the premiere of *Strange Interlude* at Grauman's Chinese Theatre in Hollywood. (Shearer was wearing a costume from *Smilin' Through*, which she had just completed.) Some of the 20,000 fans present were so excited to see Shearer and Thalberg that they broke through barricades and rushed the patio. In the resulting melee, a young woman sustained a broken leg.

1932

Nineteen thirty-two began auspiciously for Irving Thalberg, and it continued triumphantly, but it ended on notes of sadness and uncertainty. It was true that Thalberg was almost single-handedly insulating M-G-M from the depression. America was desperate. Nearly 10,000 of the country's 25,000 banks had failed. Manufacturing had plummeted to 54 percent of its 1929 level. Twelve million workers were unemployed. Even though the average movie ticket cost only a quarter, few Americans had that quarter. As a result, 8,000 of the country's 22,000 theaters had closed. With fewer outlets for their product, movie studios were feeling a pinch. Warner Bros. began the year $8 million in the hole. Fox Film was just $3 million in the red, and that was due to its theater holdings. Universal stayed in business by closing down periodically. Paramount and M-G-M were solvent, but their employees had a hard time pretending that everything was normal. "All about us was misery, the backwash of the depression," wrote Frances Marion, "and the blinds were pulled down so none of the prosperous would see the evidence of sorrow and destruction around them." How did Thalberg bring his studio an $8 million profit in the worst year of the depression? He did it by pursuing literary talent, by fostering theatrical talent, and by supplying Americans with mature movie fare.

F. Scott Fitzgerald had been the most celebrated chronicler of the Jazz Age, but by 1931 his peripatetic lifestyle, his drunken escapades, and his wife's mental illness had combined to dim his luster. He made numerous attempts to sober up and find new inspiration, but he was besieged. His wife was in an expensive sanitarium and his daughter was in an expensive school. When he was invited to join Thalberg's stable of writers, he gratefully accepted. Thalberg knew the danger of hiring novelists who had not learned to translate words into images. "Novelists and playwrights without picture experience—especially those who don't see cinema and who have never visited a studio—will be inclined to sacrifice action to dialogue," said Thalberg. He told Fitzgerald to adapt a *Saturday Evening Post* story by Katharine Brush called *Red-Headed Woman*. Fitzgerald asked his friend Dwight Taylor for advice. "He was worried about camera angles," wrote Taylor. "I pointed out that it was his dialogue and characterization that they were after." Fitzgerald applied himself as best he could. Anita Loos, his neighbor in the writers' building, saw "that apologetic humility which is characteristic of reformed drunks." He did not retain it for long. He made an ill-advised appearance at a Sunday afternoon party thrown by the Thalbergs at their new home on the Santa Monica beach. He got drunk and made a fool of himself, but not as big a fool as he did with *Red-Headed Woman*. "Scott tried to turn the silly story into a prose poem," said Thalberg, who then fired the hapless writer.

Thalberg had more than sixty writers on salary, but only a few got this type of attention. Dorothy Parker got it when she took a metal sign that read "Men" and attached it to the door of her writing cubicle. Cyril Hume got attention when he caused producer Bernard Hyman (and himself) to burst into tears by solving a script problem that had stopped *Trader Horn* in its tracks. P. G. Wodehouse, the British author of the Jeeves novels, got attention when he told the *Los Angeles Times* that M-G-M had paid him $100,000 to sit by a swimming pool and do nothing. "I was led to believe that there was a field for my work in pictures," said Wodehouse, "but I was told that my stuff was 'too light.' They seem to have such a passion for sex stuff. I wonder if they really know the tastes of their audiences." Thalberg got an angry call from Nick Schenck, to which he replied: "If you know a way to make pictures without writers, tell me!"

For the most part, though, Thalberg's stable was quiet and productive. To turn out fifty films a year, they had to be. Thalberg customarily assigned several writers to the same script. Frances Marion would come up with an idea. John Colton would break it down into a step outline. Leon Gordon would write a continuity with scenes and dialogue. Thalberg would then have a story conference with the supervisor (who was now called a "producer"), the director, and the writer (or writers) to determine where the script would go from there. Then a writer who specialized in comedy, for instance, would brighten the dialogue. Or a drama specialist like Ivor Novello would put in a moving curtain speech. "Gag-man" Robert Hopkins would go through the script putting one-liners where needed. Then another story conference would occur. Scenes would be added (or subtracted). A "final continuity" would be approved. Casting and set design would commence. Then on to the next script. In this way, Thalberg kept films rolling off the assembly line. He usually attended one

sneak preview a week, which reflected M-G-M's goal of one release a week. In 1932, because of economic conditions, and because every Thalberg film was a quality production, fewer than forty would be released.

The qualified success of *The Guardsman* and the outright hit of *Private Lives* gave Thalberg the confidence to continue with his synthesis of theater and film. Lionel Barrymore had been with M-G-M for seven years, but after winning an Academy Award for his performance in *A Free Soul*, he assumed a new significance: he was part of the royal family of Broadway. His sister Ethel had been a stage star for thirty years. His brother John had created a legendary Hamlet on Broadway eight years earlier and then became a star at Warner Bros. Putting two Barrymores in one talkie would be newsworthy. To accomplish this, Thalberg had to offer John more than Warners was paying him. John accepted and joined his brother Lionel in Culver City. The result was the witty, thrill-packed *Arsene Lupin*. If Thalberg could get two Barrymores, why not three? Broadway was having a hard time in 1932, so Thalberg went after Ethel, the "first lady" of the theater. She turned him down. So did Katharine Cornell, the "great lady" of the theater. "Each time I am here in Los Angeles," said Cornell, "I promise Irving Thalberg to make a screen test. But I never do. I just go away and send a wire filled with regrets." Thalberg then went after the "bad girl" of Broadway, Tallulah Bankhead, who was making flop after flop at Paramount. She agreed to come to M-G-M, and, although she finally had a hit (*Faithless*), she returned to the stage. When Thalberg offered Ethel Barrymore $3,000 a week and the chance to play Empress Alexandra with Lionel as Rasputin and John as a brave prince, she gave in.

Rasputin was a troubled production because Ethel had to be back on Broadway by a certain date and Thalberg started shooting before Charles MacArthur had finished his script. Fifteen script conferences, two directors, and $1.1 million later, the film called *Rasputin and the Empress* caused a mob scene at the Astor, but it lost money and became another "prestige picture." It also became the first to cause M-G-M a libel suit; the prince on whom John's character was based sued M-G-M—and won. Then a plagiarism suit was filed against M-G-M for the popular Joan Crawford film *Letty Lynton*. The playwrights of *Dishonored Lady* claimed that Thalberg had appropriated their story of the "Edinburgh poisoner." M-G-M had to pay a settlement and permanently withdraw *Letty Lynton*. Such missteps were inevitable in a year when Thalberg was defying the depression. Most of the fourteen films he made from stage plays in 1932 were profitable. Two were unusually so.

With *The Divorcee*, *A Free Soul*, *Strangers May Kiss*, and *Strange Interlude*, Thalberg had turned his wife into the "torch bearer for the single standard." The venerable play *Smilin' Through* was an odd choice for a Shearer vehicle. "After having played so many sophisticated roles," said Shearer, "I worried that my fans might find *Smilin' Through* old-fashioned and overly sentimental. It was the story of a love that transcended death, a love that connected two women who lived in two different times [1850 and 1915] and loved two different men. I told Irving that I simply couldn't play a sweet young girl of so long ago, and that I wouldn't be able to make the more modern one, Kathleen, interesting. He wisely waved my objections aside."

"Young lady," said Thalberg, "you do it and like it!" He was right about *Smilin' Through*. *Variety* reported that the adult love story "kept the audience spellbound and hushed, save for the flutter of women's handkerchiefs." *Smilin' Through* was a million-dollar hit in the grim winter of 1932.

The film that exemplified the Thalberg touch more than any other was a hybrid grown in an M-G-M hot-house. German novelist Vicki Baum wrote a book about a hotel scandal in Berlin. She even worked as a chambermaid to complete her research. When *Menschem im Hotel* was about to be mounted as a Broadway play, Thalberg stepped in and offered to back it. *Grand Hotel* paid back his investment in a week and gave him the thrill of a first-nighter. It also gave him the template for a superb crowd pleaser, a series of show-stopping scenes about five hotel guests caught in a whirlwind of events beyond their control or understanding. Such a story was gripping when enacted onstage by relatively unknown players. Thalberg looked at the characters and had a brainstorm, one that flew in the face of both studio economics and depression box office. Each character would be played by an M-G-M star. *Grand Hotel* would be the first "all-star" film. Of equal significance was Thalberg's translation of the play from stage to screen. He had his director and screenwriter Edmund Goulding avoid static two-shots, instead telling the story with bold camera angles, graceful crane shots, and rhythmic cutting. This was a far cry from the "canned theater" of which he had been accused in his early talkies. It had both cinematic integrity and the magic of live theater. With films like *Grand Hotel*, Thalberg was accomplishing his goal, the synthesis of two art forms.

If there was ever a year when it was possible for a visionary producer to introduce the public to offbeat, thoughtful, adult films, it was 1932. Will Hays had gotten Jason Joy to stop the making of crime and horror films, but he had forgotten about sex. "With crime practically denied them," recalled Joy, "with box-office figures down, with high pressure being employed back home to spur the studios on to get a little more cash, it was almost inevitable that sex, the nearest thing at hand and pretty generally surefire, should be seized on. It was." Joy did not believe in censoring for the sake of censorship; the Montana-born former Red Cross executive had a sense of humor and trusted Thalberg's good intentions. In his review of *Faithless*, Joy reasoned with Thalberg, trying to find a way to retain the truth of the plot without offending either the audience or his beleaguered former employers. "The moral issues involved are complicated by the current economic situation," Joy wrote Thalberg. "If it is to be shown that the depression has reduced women to going on the streets as prostitutes, then our whole national life is depicted at a low point. There will be justifiable resentment of this insinuation, particularly in view of the rather heroic efforts by relief organizations and the government." Joy was not reckoning on the American audience.

"Female picturegoers decide the fate of motion pictures," declared the *Exhibitors Herald-World*, "because women make up a majority of the vast motion picture public, particularly at the matinee performances." According to this trade journal, the audience was 75 percent women. "The smug and contented housewife subconsciously envies the glamour that surrounds cinema mistresses," wrote a *Variety* reporter. "Women are responsible for the ever-increasing public taste in sensationalism and sexy stuff," reported another. "Women love dirt. Nothing shocks 'em. They are also the majority readers of the tabloids, scandal sheets, flashy magazines, and erotic books."

Having spent seven years building a stable of female stars, Thalberg was well acquainted with the female quotient of his market. "Wives and shopgirls can always get their men to the movies they want to see," said Thalberg, "but a man can never get a woman to see one that doesn't interest her." If this was not confirmed by his preview audiences, it was by letters to fan magazines. "Why should producers be hobbled with various forms of censorship?" asked an Indianapolis woman. "Books on all subjects are placed within the reach of young people. Why pick on the movies?" And

a twelve-year-old boy from Joliet, Illinois, wrote: "I'm tired of hearing the phrases 'Children shouldn't see this!' and 'Children shouldn't hear that!' Children like sophisticated pictures as well as any other kind. Just look at Greta Garbo in *Mata Hari* and Norma Shearer in *Private Lives*. Are they sophisticated? And do I like them? Um-m-m!"

Thalberg was fascinated by human behavior in all its colorful manifestations, and by sex, whether normal or "inverted." The plots of *Faithless*, *Tarzan the Ape Man*, *Letty Lynton*, *Red-Headed Woman*, and *Grand Hotel* all turned on sexual tension. During a *Grand Hotel* story conference, he accused Goulding of weakening a sequence. "You've got a scene, Eddie, in which a man [John Barrymore] for two pages lies to a woman [Greta Garbo] like a so-and-so," said Thalberg. "You haven't got any sex in it."

"I'm not defending this, Irving, but—"

"When he's on a sex thing, he's perfectly within his rights. When he has seen a naked woman, he can suddenly, very honestly, have a sex desire come over him—particularly if she is a little reckless herself. Why does a woman want one man and another woman want another man? That's the kick of it, God damn it!"

Thalberg's insistence on finding the motivation of his characters was only one aspect of his quest for cinematic truth. "I have never seen a film made outside this lot that had a convincing story," he said to producer Paul Bern one day. Ironically it was Bern who caused Thalberg to step back from his tapestry of dreams and look at reality. First, *Red-Headed Woman*, which launched Bern's protégée Jean Harlow as an M-G-M star, created a furor with church men and club women because its predatory heroine was allowed to sin graphically and without retribution. Next, the middle-aged Bern, a confirmed bachelor who was known as a self-conscious do-gooder, married the young and nubile Harlow. Two months later, Bern shot himself, and a traumatized Harlow became the focal point of a scandal. Thalberg was himself numb with grief at the death of his closest advisor, but he managed to help Louis B. Mayer order the investigation and save Harlow's nascent career.

The Bern tragedy came in the middle of a journalistic investigation by *Fortune* magazine. The result was a widely read article. It characterized Mayer as a "commercial diplomat" who dealt in "contracts, contacts . . . personal connections, intrigues, and affiliations." By contrast, *Fortune* declared: "Irving Thalberg, a small and fragile young man with a suggestion of anemia, is . . . what Hollywood means by M-G-M." Predictably, this stuck in Mayer's craw, and, when Thalberg, bereft of motivation for the first time in his meteoric career, came to him and threatened to quit, Mayer assumed it was yet another ploy to get a raise. He set his jaw, took his own counsel, and then stood by while Thalberg waged a week-long battle with Nick Schenck—and won.

Loew's granted Thalberg an extended contract and a very generous 100,000-share stock option. Mayer only got 80,000. Two months later, as 1932 came to a close, it became known that the studio would reap a profit of $8 million. In spite of everything it had been a banner year, a tribute to Thalberg's taste and diligence. The thirty-three-year-old vice president in charge of production had a few well-deserved drinks at the studio Christmas party, but, as always, he celebrated temperately. His body did not agree. A few days after Christmas, he suffered his second heart attack. Several days later his doctors pronounced him out of danger, but he could not return to work. While he lay in his soundproofed, air-conditioned bedroom on New Year's Eve, contemplating his future with M-G-M, Mayer decided where it lay.

Charles Brabin's *The Beast of the City* was a crime film starring Walter Huston, but sexy scenes between Wallace Ford and Jean Harlow (seen here) sold theater tickets. Thalberg took note of Harlow's popularity and signed her to a contract a few months later.

The most eagerly awaited, innovative, and successful film of 1932 was Edmund Goulding's *Grand Hotel*, the first "all-star" film. This scene shows Joan Crawford, John Barrymore, Lionel Barrymore, and Lewis Stone in the lounge called the Yellow Room.

Skyscraper Souls was a multi-character drama in the *Grand Hotel* mold, but without stars. It had several standout scenes, including this one, in which Warren William (left) and George Barbier ply Maureen O'Sullivan with champagne. *Skyscraper Souls* was one of Thalberg's best films in his best year, but the depression kept it from becoming a hit.

Opposite: One of Thalberg's most enduring contributions to popular culture was the casting of Olympic champion Johnny Weissmuller as Edgar Rice Burroughs's Tarzan. Thalberg called his version of the Burroughs franchise *Tarzan the Ape Man*. "'Gawd, whadda physique!'" began an article by Ida Zeitlin. "Eyes glowing, cheeks scarlet, lips parted, aged about seventeen, she sat on the edge of her seat in the movie theatre, unconscious of the people about her, unconscious that she had spoken, unconscious of everything but the young god on the screen before her. Torn from her by sheer intensity of feeling, her ecstatic tribute was breathed forth upon the listening air—not to mention several pairs of appreciative ears: 'Gawd, whadda physique!'" Photograph by George Hurrell, courtesy hurrellphotos.com; negative printed by the author

Grand Hotel had a conspicuous but unbilled star: the hotel itself. "Here the sets take the place of an actor in the story," said art director Cedric Gibbons. "The Grand Hotel is bigger than the people who come and go through its doors." Photograph by Clarence Bull

Thalberg's judgment failed in the final editing of the fight scene between Beery and John Barrymore. Thalberg thought that Barrymore looked "petty" whacking Beery on the arm (just before Beery brutally beats him with a telephone). Thalberg ordered that Barrymore's action be cut, but there was no coverage of an alternate angle. The result was a jump cut that looked like something had been censored.

This *Grand Hotel* scene between Garbo and John Barrymore had already been shot twice because Thalberg decided that it had bad cutting. "You want to be on her when you are on him," he told Goulding. "The angle should be on both of them." Garbo and Barrymore returned for retakes on a scene that would eventually be censored in Philadelphia. "I wish something could be done about the censors in our city," wrote a woman in that city. "*Grand Hotel* was ruined by having much conversation eliminated. When the picture was cut, some of the audience imagined things worse than they were."

"The director is on the set to communicate what I expect of the actors," said Thalberg. "It has been my experience that directors realize only seventy-five percent of our scenarios, and while the audience never knows how much it has missed, I do." Edmund Goulding's handling of the scenes between John Barrymore and Joan Crawford came close to realizing 100 percent of the scenario he wrote with Thalberg.

Marie Dressler became M-G-M's number one star in 1932, thanks to the vulgar, funny *Prosperity*, one of the few Thalberg films to address the Great Depression. Photograph by Clarence Bull

In this scene from *Red-Headed Woman*, the vulgar, scheming Lil seduces her boss (Chester Morris) in a roadhouse phone booth. A *Variety* reviewer reported opening night reactions. "There was light, scattered laughter at the torrid episodes, and, once or twice, when the red-headed sister had to take it on the chin, there was a faint stir of approval. But whether they were moved to laughter or audible approval, the flaps (flappers; i.e., young girls) showed every manifestation of interest." After heated negotiations with industry censors, Thalberg's racy film became the most controversial of 1932.

Opposite: Jean Harlow, the famed "Platinum Blonde," began her M-G-M contract in a red wig to gain the coveted role of Lil Andrews in *Red-Headed Woman*. Hurrell's frankly sexual portraits of Harlow did much to publicize the film. Photograph by George Hurrell, courtesy hurrellphotos.com

To quell rumors of mutual hatred, Norma Shearer and Joan Crawford posed for press photographers at the November 1932 Mayfair Ball. (Thalberg was dancing, meanwhile, with his old flame, Rosabelle Laemmle.) "Why Norma and Joan were at odds I wasn't sure," recalled Helen Hayes, who was close to both. "Surely they couldn't have been rivals for the same roles."

Opposite: *Letty Lynton* brought Crawford to the apex of her popularity as a Thalberg star. Portrait by George Hurrell

Crawford went from *Grand Hotel* to *Letty Lynton*, a glamour vehicle with Robert Montgomery and Nils Asther (seen here). Donovan Pedelty of *Silver Screen* magazine visited the *Letty Lynton* set to describe this Montevideo nightclub scene. "Forty ripe-looking couples are dancing the tango in forty square feet of café. They sway like one jellyfish. Offset two grips burn sulphur cloth and fan its acrid smoke towards the camera to thicken the atmosphere. Nils Asther, in white trousers and a moiré tuxedo, a feminine-pulse-stirring figure, is dancing with Joan Crawford. Naturally he kisses her, and naturally she likes it." Photograph by Sam Manatt

The Mask of Fu Manchu was a successful horror entry, even if some audiences found its gruesome excesses more funny than scary. Myrna Loy played Fu Manchu's "ugly and insignificant" daughter with wicked abandon.

Tony Gaudio's camerawork and Cedric Gibbons's art direction made *The Mask of Fu Manchu* look like an opium dream. Boris Karloff made Dr. Fu Manchu sound like a lisping serpent.

With Marion Davies (left) as a slum girl who becomes a Ziegfeld showgirl and Billie Dove (far right) as her fair-weather friend, Edmund Goulding's *Blondie of the Follies* was a charming film. It could have been a great film if William Randolph Hearst had not forced Thalberg to cut Dove's best scenes (because they upstaged Davies). Photograph by James Manatt

After five flops at Paramount, Tallulah Bankhead was ready to return to Broadway, but Thalberg talked her into making an M-G-M movie. *Faithless* had its share of retakes and cut scenes (including this one), but it proved that a Bankhead film could make money, even in the worst year of the depression.

Alexander Kirkland and Norma Shearer played blissful newlyweds in Thalberg's very free adaptation of Eugene O'Neill's *Strange Interlude*. Shearer confounded critics with a convincing portrayal of an aging neurotic. Photograph by William Grimes

Tod Browning's *Freaks* was meant to be Thalberg's answer to *Frankenstein*, but it became a corporate horror story. Intensely hostile reactions in every major city prompted M-G-M to withdraw the film from circulation before it had completed its exhibition contracts. In this scene, Prince Randian, the Human Torso (playing himself), shows Rollo Brother (Matt McHugh) how to light a cigarette without using his hands.

A *Freaks* group portrait: (from left) unidentified player, Johnny Eck, Jenny Lee Snow, Elvira Snow, Tod Browning, Schlitze, Peter Robinson, Minnie Woolsey, Josephine Joseph, and Olga Roderick.

In this scene from *Freaks*, Cleopatra the Aerialist (Olga Baclanova) pays the penalty for violating the code of the freaks.

Casting the three Barrymore siblings in *Rasputin* promised to be Thalberg's triumph of 1932. Lionel, Ethel, and John Barrymore sat for a historic portrait on the *Rasputin* set in late July. "As I looked at them through my camera," wrote Clarence Bull in 1968, "I got the shock of my life. They all looked alike. All looked alike, no matter how I posed them. The bond between them was both amazing and frightening."

Rasputin also had a totally fictitious scene in which the "holy man" tries to seduce Princess Maria (Jean Parker).

RASPUTIN: I heard you went to the hospital today.

MARIA (sadly): Yes. Mother and I talked to a boy . . . the first day he was at the front, he lost both his hands. And he was so brave . . . and beautiful.

RASPUTIN (intrigued): Do you like beautiful boys?

MARIA: I don't know what you mean, Father.

RASPUTIN: Oh, that's all right. It's perfectly natural for girls to think of boys. You must never be ashamed of life, my dear. Never.

Possessed had been a breakthrough for Crawford and Clark Gable, but British censors refused to play it. After a year, Thalberg decided to shoot a scene in which Gable offers to make her an honest woman. The scene was shot in October 1932, and Crawford's hair and makeup did not match scenes shot a year earlier, but no one in London complained.

Following the notoriety of *Red-Headed Woman*, Jean Harlow was urged to pose seductively. Photograph by Russell Ball

Opposite: After Jean Harlow married producer Paul Bern, her portraits took on a dignified tone. Studio publicists tried anything and everything in an effort to present Miss Harlow as Mrs. Bern. Photograph by Clarence Bull

Making Harlow look sedate was forgotten when *Red Dust* went into production. Clarence Bull told Harlow and Gable to "heat up the negative." A month later, Paul Bern committed suicide, and the ensuing scandal threatened Harlow's career.

No taint touched Clark Gable, whose star continued upward. While he cut a fine figure in a suit, his image was based on his ease with mechanics and hunting. Films like *Strange Interlude* (in which he played a doctor) were put aside in favor of rough-and-tumble outings like *Red Dust*. Photograph by Clarence Bull

Opposite: At Greta Garbo's command, Thalberg allowed Erich von Stroheim to return to M-G-M for the first time in seven years. He acted with her in *As You Desire Me* (shown here). After a few more frustrating years in Hollywood, Stroheim went to Europe.

Above: Jean Harlow's popularity survived the scandalous death of her husband. Portrait by George Hurrell

Opposite: This Hurrell portrait of Crawford in *Letty Lynton* ran as an exclusive in *Screenland,* undoubtedly contributing to the film's half-million-dollar profit.

Above: George Hurrell made this *Strange Interlude* portrait of Norma Shearer in May 1932.

Howard Hawks's *Today We Live* was adapted by William Faulkner from his World War I novel *Turn About*. When Thalberg looked at Faulkner's script, he said: "I'd leave tracks all over it if I tried to improve it. Go ahead and shoot it as it stands." Mayer decided that Joan Crawford should be added to the cast, so Faulkner's aviation story became a Crawford vehicle. Crawford had just given a powerful but unappreciated performance in *Rain*. *Today We Live* also flopped, and her career went into a slump. Photograph by Frank Tanner

1933

January 1933 was a strange time at M-G-M. For the first time since its founding, Irving Thalberg was not at the studio, looking in on projects, guiding, advising, inspiring. He was at home, recovering from a heart attack. For the first time since Mission Road, Louis B. Mayer was involving himself in production. He was discovering that while he was not especially suited to the creative end of the business, he enjoyed contact with his studio "family." Thalberg's producers were religiously methodical, so his absence caused no hiccup in the assembly line. Mayer took note of this, and, swallowing his pride, made overtures to Nick Schenck. In early February, they dropped a bomb on Thalberg. David Selznick would be coming to M-G-M as an independent producer. He would be paid $4,000 a week (twice Paul Bern's salary) to supervise six pictures a year and would answer only to Mayer, who happened to be his father-in-law. But this was not the worst of it. Thalberg's production system was being reorganized. Henceforth, there would be a "unit system" of six "executive producers."

Thalberg did not wait to find out if he would be overseeing them. In late February, he left for Europe with his wife and son, ostensibly to consult Dr. Franz Groedel in Bad Nauheim, Germany. Shearer had agreed to a hiatus, assuring Thalberg that his health was more important than her career. The Thalbergs were accompanied by Charles MacArthur, Helen Hayes, and their young daughter, Mary (whom Irving Jr. called his girlfriend). While the celebrated travelers sailed through the Panama Canal, their country went through a series of upheavals.

With 15 million Americans out of work, the depression had reached a critical stage. The previous November's presidential election had been described by Herbert Hoover as "a contest between two philosophies of government." Franklin D. Roosevelt's philosophy of courage had won, but, as his inauguration approached, many people wondered if the brave rescue would arrive in time. Frightened bank depositors were rushing their branches, only to be met by padlocked doors. (A nervous Helen Hayes was carrying cash on her trip, which caused Thalberg to chide her.) To forestall disaster, banks began exporting gold. Some states tried to stabilize the situation by declaring emergency bank holidays. It was no use. The American banking system was on the verge of collapse. Roosevelt's March 4 inauguration provided another day off. Once in office, he ordered a three-day bank holiday. Thalberg was in Havana, trying in vain to cash a traveler's check. "And how does my cash look to you now?" Hayes asked him. "You wouldn't be able to buy a postcard without it."

Things got worse before they got better. On March 8, the studio heads joined to "ask" their employees to take voluntary pay cuts of 50 percent. Fearful contractees complied. On Friday, March 10, an earthquake centered in Huntington Beach rocked all of Southern California; one hundred deaths in Long Beach led to the misnomer "The Long Beach Earthquake." On Monday, March 13, striking laborers closed every Hollywood studio. The Academy of Motion Picture Arts and Sciences had to negotiate a sliding scale to exempt employees making $50 or less from the "voluntary" pay cuts. Thalberg was in New York during the controversy, and he criticized Mayer and Schenck before he departed for Europe. The respective heads of the Mayer and Loew's groups responded to his criticism by uniting against him. While he was in Bad Nauheim having his tonsils removed, Schenck approached every producer whom Thalberg had groomed, offering executive producer status—and screen credit. Only Albert Lewin declined. Mayer added three more producers. He and Schenck were ready to show their hand. Thalberg was recuperating at the Hôtel du Cap, outside Antibes, when he received a cable from Mayer. It informed him that M-G-M now comprised eight executive producers. The post of vice president in charge of production had been eliminated. Thalberg was hereby relieved of his duties. Mayer ended the cable with the phrase: "Am doing this for you."

Thalberg wisely refrained from rushing to answer or return. He spent two more months in Europe, enjoying England and Scotland, before sailing to New York to meet with Schenck. Once there, he went to Schenck's Long Island mansion for a series of surprisingly productive talks. Thalberg was willing to become part of the new system as long as he did not have to answer to Mayer, whom he felt had used his illness to seize control. Schenck was as sympathetic as a conflict of interest would permit. "Isn't it better, Irving, that you make just the films you like to make?" he asked. "You can do all of Norma's films, and five or six specials besides." Thalberg knew who he was dealing with, the man who had sold

Loew's to William Fox, but he had to consider Shearer's career. What could he do? Go to work for Sam Goldwyn? Give up the stars he had made—Gable, Crawford, Garbo, Beery, Dressler? Try to find backing for his own company? No, it was too much to contemplate. He signed with M-G-M. He would be an executive producer with his own building.

Back in Culver City, he was greeted by a justifiably happy Mayer and duly installed in a temporary office while a splendid bungalow was prepared. Within a month he was being subtly stonewalled. "The difficulties I encounter," he wrote Schenck, "are an inability to acquire talent and an inability to make that talent give its best efforts. The first is due to the fact that unless I wish to exercise the rights under my contract, I cannot get a first-class person who is employed on this lot." The very stars he had raised from obscurity to celebrity were suddenly unavailable for the projects he was preparing. To appease him, Schenck called Mayer, who answered: "Thalberg wants first call on every artist on the lot! I told him: 'Irving, I will have to throw up my hands! You ought to be fair! You are going to place me in a position where I will flop! You know that I will try to give you every darned thing that you want, as if you were my own son. But I have *got* to run this plant successfully!'" Thalberg was not interested in being Mayer's son, any more than Mayer was interested in having the producer act like the vice president he used to be. This was the problem. Mayer wanted to be appreciated. Thalberg wanted to make films his own way. Neither man would acknowledge the other's needs.

After two months of being unable to get even the writers he wanted, Thalberg found a way around the stone wall. Ensconced in the oak-paneled interior of his new bungalow, he commissioned Edmund Goulding to write and direct a sexy vehicle for Norma Shearer. Little by little, Thalberg got the cooperation he required.

Metro-Goldwyn-Mayer Studios had grown to fifty-three acres by 1933, a sizable battleground for the well-matched egos of Louis B. Mayer and Irving Thalberg. This aerial photograph shows Lot One. The corner of Washington Boulevard and Overland Avenue is in the foreground.

Schenck got him permission to sign talent exclusively to his production unit. He was the only M-G-M producer given the privilege of personal contracts. He quickly signed up Sidney Franklin, Donald Ogden Stewart, Preston Sturges, Ernest Vajda, Claudine West, and Frances Marion. With numerous scripts in preparation and a film finally in production, Thalberg ended 1933 on a note of optimism, one shared by M-G-M. The films Thalberg had begun in 1932 helped the studio achieve a profit of $4 million. Loew's shareholders received their dividends. M-G-M employees had salaries restored to their former levels. However, salary cuts were not reimbursed, even though the Mayer Group did manage to make up its loss, and Thalberg continued to share in its profits. He had flirted with socialism as a teenager but had become a staunch capitalist, and, although he was unceasingly kind to underlings, no egalitarian impulse would deprive him of his dividends.

When all was said and done, Thalberg had survived both the worst year of the depression and the corporate equivalent of a palace coup. Yet he persisted with his faith in the industry and his commitment to its product. "Nobody has ever been able to say definitely whether picture making is really a business or an art," wrote Thalberg. "Personally, I think it is both. It is a business in the sense that it must bring in money at the box office, but it is an art in that it involves, from its devotees, the inexorable demands of creative expression. In short, it is a creative business, dependent, as almost no other business is, on the emotional reaction of its customers." If his new production unit was to succeed, Thalberg would need to get that reaction.

Thalberg sent director W. S. ("Woody") Van Dyke to Alaska to film Peter Freuchen's book *Esquimaux*, but did not expect Van Dyke to cast himself (at left), Freuchen, and Ray Wise (right) in the film. Wise was a Russian-Jewish-Eskimo native of Nome. He filled in when Van Dyke's lead actor disappeared. Wise changed his name to Mala and returned to Hollywood with Van Dyke to work as an actor (and assistant cameraman). *Eskimo* was released in late 1933 after much reshooting. Fine as it was, it could not recoup the cost of location work and studio retakes.

Thalberg's production of *Pig Boats* was planned for Wallace Beery and Clark Gable, but, by the time it reached the screen, it starred Walter Huston and Robert Montgomery, and was called *Hell Below*. It also featured Jimmy Durante and a boxing kangaroo.

Opposite: Another 1932 Thalberg project released during his 1933 absence was *The Secret of Madame Blanche*. It featured Irene Dunne, who was not yet a star, and Phillips Holmes.

Greta Garbo and John Gilbert were reunited in *Queen Christina*, a project begun by Thalberg but produced by Walter Wanger. When Thalberg returned to the studio, director Rouben Mamoulian screened the first cut for him. "This is a great film," Thalberg told him. "But you could make it a greater film if you spend another $200,000." Mamoulian reshot the ending and created an enduring classic. Photograph by Milton Brown

After a year off the screen, Norma Shearer needed to decide on a vehicle. Should she try a Broadway play like Michael Arlen's *The Green Hat*, Stefan Zweig's book *Marie Antoinette*, or an original story by Edmund Goulding? While pondering her options, she posed for portraits that portrayed her as the first lady of M-G-M, recently returned from a royal tour. Her box-office standing had not been affected by her absence. It was generally known that she put her husband's health ahead of her career from genuine concern, not *noblesse oblige*. Photograph by George Hurrell

On December 19, 1933, Thalberg was photographed in his living room. The uncredited photographer captured his hypnotic gaze. "He had terrific eyes," wrote Walter Wanger years later. "You thought that you were talking to an Indian savant. He could cast a spell on anybody." The serenity in Thalberg's eyes is all the more remarkable for the battles that he was fighting when this portrait was made.

Thalberg's first film as an independent producer at M-G-M was *Riptide*, in which Shearer added another portrait to her gallery of free souls. "Since women have found and tasted their new freedom," said Shearer, "I don't believe that they will ever give it up. Various people have predicted a return to almost mid-Victorian conventions. They say that the pendulum of public opinion is bound to swing backward. But I don't think that women will ever go back to the old prewar restrictions on thought and action. Women have tasted freedom and they like it." Photograph by George Hurrell

1934

Thalberg's first film as an independent producer at M-G-M should have been a simple proposition. Because he was dealing with both art and politics, it was not. Mayer had blocked Thalberg's access to every worthwhile M-G-M director, so he had to consider freelancers. He had a happy history with Edmund Goulding, who had directed the super-hit *Grand Hotel* in early 1932 and *Blondie of the Follies* in mid-1932. Thalberg wanted Goulding, but the director was blacklisted because of something he had directed in September 1932: an orgy. In a letter to Noël Coward, Adela Rogers St. Johns relayed the gossip. "Eddie Goulding left here on twelve hours' notice," wrote St. Johns, "after giving a party for eight girls which wound up with two of them having to be sent to the hospital. Hearst stepped in and squashed the story. One of the newspapers told the studio people not to worry about the story being printed as it was so filthy it couldn't be." Just how filthy was it? The owner of Goulding's rented home sued him for damage to carpets, red leather cushions, and an axe.

In spite of both the Production Code and the depression, Hollywood films—and Hollywood—had gotten filthy, too. *Red-Headed Woman* had opened the door for unabashedly adult films such as *Call Her Savage*, *The Sign of the Cross*, and *She Done Him Wrong*. Will Hays had managed to stave off criticism while the film capital was reeling from earthquakes, strikes, and bankruptcy, but his platitudes were wearing thin. Reformers and congressmen alike were calling for an end to "immoral" movies. At one point Hays had sent a pugnacious Catholic named Joseph I. Breen to check up on the SRC. Breen was not impressed with Jason Joy's efforts and found Hollywood mores repugnant. "Here we have paganism rampant and in its most virulent form," Breen wrote Hays. "Drunkenness and debauchery are commonplace. Sexual perversion is rampant, and any number of our prominent stars and directors are perverts."

In the front ranks of these perverts was the bisexual Goulding, a well-known patron of drag shows starring Jean Malin and the Rocky Twins at the Ship Café in Venice; he even cast the twins in *Blondie of the Follies*, although he stopped short of putting the androgynous performers in dresses. In late 1933, Thalberg got Goulding off the blacklist and onto the M-G-M payroll. Goulding repaid Thalberg's loyalty with an original story called *Rip-tide*. Norma Shearer's first film in eighteen months would be the morality tale of an American girl who marries a British lord and then dallies with an American playboy. This was a return to the formula of *The Divorcee*, *Strangers May Kiss*, and *A Free Soul*, Thalberg told the press. Apparently someone had misgivings about such fare when Hollywood was being censured for a surfeit of sex, so Shearer gave a series of interviews.

"Sophistication should not suggest vulgarity," Shearer explained. "It should be translated into characterizations of worldly wisdom, modern thinking, and resolute freedom. After all, conventions are man-made laws. Like all laws, they are constantly changing to meet new standards. We wear our conventions the way we wear these clothes. With dignity, but with a touch of daring. Show me the woman who does not like to appear a trifle—well, shall we say daring—just every once in a while." She reassured another reporter of her innate conservatism. "Women have learned how to manage their new freedom," said Shearer. "In those early days, everything was so new that we overplayed our independence from conventions. We tried to be masculine and we succeeded in being only foolishly obvious. Women today are having careers, going places, and doing things, but they still are managing to be good wives and mothers. A woman can be free and independent, can act and think as she pleases, without losing a bit of feminine charm." In Goulding's story, Lady Mary Rexford must reconcile a free-spirited flirtation with its potential damage to her home life. The problem with Shearer playing this part was that she was, in fact, a career woman who was also a wife and mother; unlike Lady Mary, she was above reproach.

Against his better judgment, Thalberg started shooting before Goulding had finished his script. Goulding was also directing, and he never managed to catch up. *Rip-tide* became *Lady Mary's Lover* and then *Riptide* without ever gaining the unity for which Thalberg's films were famous. *Riptide* had other problems: its early scenes did not show the rapport between Lady Mary and her husband (Herbert Marshall), and the film lacked the "one great scene" that made a great Thalberg film. Most reviews praised Shearer. Her acting had a new authority and resonance. Every review decried Thalberg's choice of vehicle. Although he still did not put his name in the credits, he did allow it at the bottom of full-page magazine ads: "An Irving Thalberg Production." With Thalberg as a fully visible target, the ever-tart *Time*

magazine took aim. "A year and a half ago," wrote an uncredited sniper, "Norma Shearer's wiry little husband, Irving Thalberg, Hollywood's No. 1 producer, suffered the nervous breakdown which for his profession is almost an occupational disease. . . . Fully recovered, Producer Thalberg finally found it possible to effect his plan of giving his personal attention to a dozen or so pictures a year, instead of supervising M-G-M's whole schedule. *Riptide* is not a good advertisement for the Thalberg plan. It is an anecdote with elephantiasis, glossy but erroneous." In spite of such reviews, *Riptide* earned a profit of $333,000. It could have earned twice that. President Roosevelt's programs had improved the economy. Weekly movie attendance had rebounded to almost 70 million. But *Riptide* ran afoul of a moral crusade.

Joseph Breen was now in charge of the SRC. The belligerent bureaucrat was a man on a mission, arguing with producers over cuts and using his unique vantage point to inform a coalition of angry Catholics. He was, in essence, a double agent for the Catholic Church. Midwest bishops, empowered by a grassroots organization called the Catholic Legion of Decency, used Breen's intelligence to fan the flames of anti-Hollywood sentiment. "It seems typical of Hollywood morality that a husband as production manager should constantly cast his wife in the role of a loose and immoral woman," wrote Father Daniel Lord in his *The Queen's Work*. "We advise strong guard over all pictures which feature Norma Shearer. They are doing more than almost any other type of picture to undermine the moral code and the Producers' Code." Thalberg angrily demanded that Los Angeles Bishop Joseph Cantwell silence Father Lord, but the damage was done. "It's a shame to ruin Shearer in this kind of story regardless of how elaborate they produce it," wrote an exhibitor in Smithville, Texas. "It will draw plenty criticism from the church people." An exhibitor in Conway, New Hampshire, was equally opprobrious. "An adult attraction," he snorted. "We hope that the churches will make Hollywood producers understand that what theaters want is good clean pictures."

Thalberg's second independent production, *The Barretts of Wimpole Street*, was barely under way when the so-called Bishops' Revolt took place. Cued by Breen, bishops in major Midwest and Eastern cities began preaching abstinence from movies, and not just sinful movies—all movies. America's Catholic population of 20 million was concentrated in the same cities where the film industry had its most profitable picture palaces. In May, Philadelphia's Denis Cardinal Dougherty exhorted his parishioners to boycott all Hollywood movies under threat of mortal sin. In less than a week, box-office receipts dropped 40 percent. By mid-June, Hollywood was out several million dollars. Only a year after the bank crisis, few studios had enough capital to last more than two weeks, and the Catholic owners of the Bank of America would not lend money for immoral movies. Hollywood had to wave the white flag. When

the smoke cleared, the landscape had been altered. There was an enforceable Production Code, the Studio Relations Committee had become the Production Code Administration (PCA), and Joseph Breen was its boss. His office opened for business on July 11.

The Barretts of Wimpole Street had slid through the SRC in February while Breen was politicking on the East Coast. This was the Katharine Cornell play about Elizabeth Barrett's rescue from oppression by the dashing poet Robert Browning. What the SRC had missed was the play's sexual subtext. The oppression came from Barrett's father, whose interest in her was distinctly unfatherly. Thalberg made certain that the theme of incest was suggested, but ever so slightly. Charles Laughton, who was playing Papa Barrett, told Thalberg: "They won't be able to censor the glint in my eye." Laughton was suddenly disingenuous when the *Los Angeles Times* brought up the story's "outré suggestion of irregularity." He denied it, saying it was only the "affectionate bond existing between father and child." Before it could be filmed, *The Barretts of*

Irving Thalberg and Norma Shearer were photographed on the deck of Joseph Schenck's yacht *Invader* in October 1934. A month later, Norma was pregnant with their second child.

Wimpole Street encountered another roadblock. William Randolph Hearst wanted it for Marion Davies. Thalberg had to bait Hearst with another property so that Shearer could play Barrett. A few months later, the same thing happened with *Marie Antoinette*, a biography Thalberg had been developing for Shearer. This time Mayer had to step in and gamble his immensely valuable connection with the Hearst press. Surprisingly, Mayer put Thalberg's interests ahead of his own and refused to let Hearst have *Marie Antoinette*. After nine years at M-G-M, Hearst canceled his contract with Mayer, moved Cosmopolitan Pictures to Warner Bros., and banned Shearer's name from his papers. Shearer eventually took an olive branch to Davies, and the Hearst press resumed coverage of M-G-M films, but Davies remained at Warners, where she quietly ended her career several years later.

The Barretts of Wimpole Street became the hit that Thalberg needed to demonstrate his independence. His next film, though, suffered the strictures of Breen's new regime. *Outcast Lady* was a remake of the 1929 Greta Garbo film *A Woman of Affairs*, which, in turn, was based on the racy Michael Arlen best-seller *The Green Hat*. There was no way that Breen was going to allow Thalberg to film the story of a woman whose groom jumps out of a window on their wedding night because he has syphilis. The film that resulted was a series of brittle vignettes. Because Thalberg still could not get the big M-G-M stars he wanted, he borrowed Constance Bennett from Darryl Zanuck's new company, Twentieth Century Pictures. Bennett was the definition of soignée but miscast as a Lost Generation martyr; she looked too glamorous to be destroyed by love. *Outcast Lady* was a flop. So was the Helen Hayes vehicle *What Every Woman Knows*. Thalberg made the mistake of trying to tamper with a play by Sir James Barrie that Hayes had made a Broadway hit. It lost everything in translation— its whimsy, its charm, and its box-office potential.

The 1934 project that most excited Thalberg was the remake of his 1925 hit *The Merry Widow*. This time, instead of Erich von Stroheim's wicked cynicism, it would have the "Lubitsch touch." Ernst Lubitsch was the Paramount director responsible for the purely cinematic innuendo that had made hit after hit—and had made stars of Jeanette MacDonald and Maurice Chevalier. Thalberg's concept was to bring Paramount's team intact to M-G-M and have the songwriting team of Richard Rodgers and Lorenz Hart adapt Franz Lehar's songs to MacDonald's vocal requirements. As Thalberg expected, Lubitsch made the sentimental operetta a delicately sexy affair, laced with humor and grace. No one expected Martin Quigley, editor of the *Exhibitor's Herald*, to go on the offensive when he attended the New York premiere of *The Merry Widow*. Quigley denounced Thalberg for having "introduced a lot of filth" into a beloved musical and threatened Breen with the loss of his job.

Thalberg asked Hays for help. "While I reiterate promises made to you over the telephone," wrote Thalberg, "I again plead with you to help save this picture from being made jumpy and choppy wherever possible. It was made in the best of faith and $100,000 at least was spent in making retakes to avoid every possible expense [of local censor cuts]. If these men [Quigley, Lord, and Breen] are our friends, I am sure they would not use threats nor turn on us at the first opportunity. . . . In the long run, no one will be served by vicious attacks." Hays was not immune to these attacks himself. He denied Thalberg's request. In the end Thalberg had to cut thirteen items from the film's negative. When *The Merry Widow* went into general release, the cuts were not the problem; the film's whopping budget was. It lost $113,000. It was the third of five Thalberg films to fail in 1934. It did not matter that two of these films were works of cinematic art. Thalberg needed to prove that he had not lost his touch.

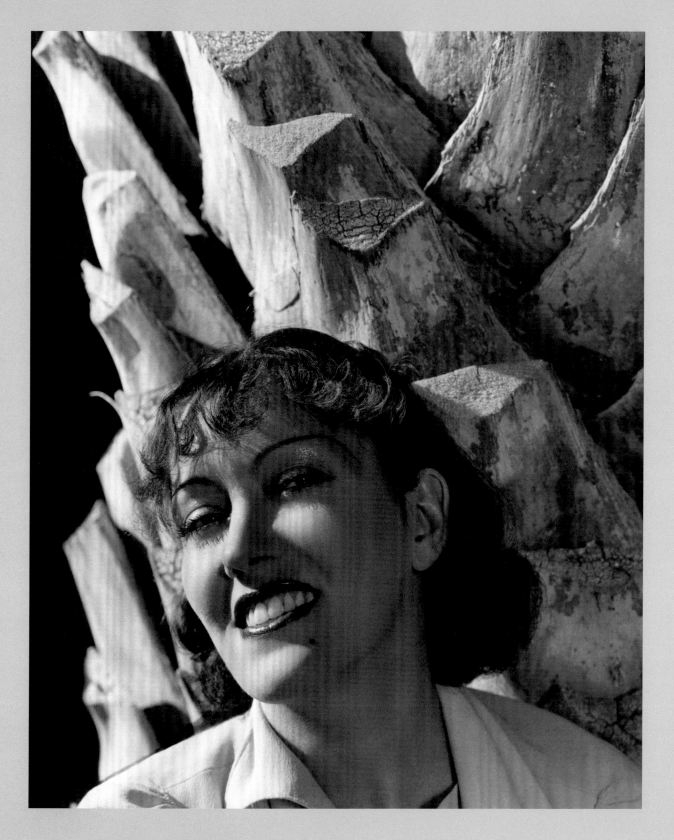

Gloria Swanson was a superstar at Liberty when Thalberg signed her to a personal contract. No other M-G-M producer was allowed to sign actors or writers to personal contracts. Portraits like these whetted the public's appetite for a Swanson epic produced by Thalberg. Photograph by Clarence Bull

Opposite: F. Scott Fitzgerald woke Irving Thalberg one night in 1934 to pitch him his new novel *Tender Is the Night* over the telephone. "Great for Norma Shearer," said Fitzgerald, but Thalberg was already filming *Riptide*. Fitzgerald was right; Shearer could have portrayed the glittering, driven Nicole. Photograph by George Hurrell

Above: *The Barretts of Wimpole Street* was the hit that established Thalberg as an independent producer. Its success was due in no small part to Shearer's restrained, authoritative performance. Photograph by Milton Brown

Constance Bennett was a showstopper in this Adrian gown, but there was no show to stop in *Outcast Lady*, Thalberg's biggest flop of 1934. Photograph by Clarence Bull

Charles MacArthur and Helen Hayes were photographed on the set of *What Every Woman Knows,* the Thalberg production that soured them on Hollywood.

Una Merkel and Ernst Lubitsch pose with the drolly suggestive bed designed by Gabriel Scognamillo for *The Merry Widow*. Photograph by Milton Brown

Milton Brown made this *Merry Widow* production still of Ernst Lubitsch, Jeanette MacDonald, and Maurice Chevalier interpreting "The Merry Widow Waltz." Thalberg fought the reconstituted Code to preserve the integrity of Lubitsch's masterpiece.

As glamorous as any M-G-M star, Thalberg posed for press photographers on May 6, 1934, with Jean Harlow and Norma Shearer at the wedding of actress Carmelita Geraghty and screenwriter Carey Wilson.

Hollywood insiders assumed that Thalberg had purchased the play *No More Ladies* for Norma Shearer. Imagine their shock when he gave it to her rival Joan Crawford, shown here dancing with Robert Montgomery. One critic wrote: "Mr. Montgomery is pretending to be a fabulous blend of Rudolph Valentino and Peter Pan." At right are Edward H. Griffith and crew members. Photograph by Frank Tanner

1935

The costume picture was the newest Hollywood trend in 1935. Cecil B. DeMille's *Cleopatra* had done well in 1934, along with Rouben Mamoulian's *Queen Christina* and Victor Fleming's *Treasure Island*. *The Barretts of Wimpole Street* had done well enough to keep Norma Shearer in the top ten. Literary classics such as *Les Miserables* and *A Tale of Two Cities* cost a story department nothing and offered no censorship problems. And there was an audience. Unemployment had dropped to 20 percent, and movie attendance had risen to 80 million a week. M-G-M had ended 1934 with a profit of $7.5 million, so Thalberg was looking for a property that would yield a blockbuster like *Ben-Hur*. He did not find it in the studio research library but in the possession of Frank Lloyd, the Academy Award-winning director of Fox Film's *Cavalcade*. Lloyd wanted to turn a novel about a South Seas mutiny into an epic film, but Fox could not afford it; that studio was on its last legs, in spite of having three of *Film Daily*'s "Top Ten" movie stars—Will Rogers, Janet Gaynor, and Shirley Temple. Lloyd would have to find backing elsewhere.

Mutiny on the Bounty was the best-seller by Charles Nordhoff and James Norman Hall. The roles of the tyrannical Captain Bligh and the mutineer Fletcher Christian would be perfect for Wallace Beery and Clark Gable—except that Lloyd wanted to play Bligh and Gable wanted no part of a period film. To get the property, Thalberg had to sell Lloyd on Beery and Gable on costumes.

"Look, Irving," said Gable. "I'm a realistic kind of actor. I've never played in a costume picture in my life. Now you want me to wear a pigtail and velvet knee pants and shoes with silver buckles. The audience will laugh me off the screen!"

To win Gable over, Thalberg enlisted the aid of Kate Corbaley. "Don't be such a mule!" Corbaley told Gable. "Listen," she said, relating the maritime tale in vivid, graphic language. "It's going to be a big picture," she concluded, "and you'll be its hero, not its heavy. How can you lose?" When Thalberg promised Gable that he would never again ask him to play a part he did not want, Gable gave in.

Thalberg had become friends with Charles Laughton while working with him on *The Barretts*. The two men could often be seen walking along Santa Monica beach on Sunday mornings, passing the mansions belonging to Thalberg's neighbors—Marion Davies, Douglas Fairbanks, and Louis B. Mayer. After discussing film theory with Laughton, Thalberg decided to take the juicy part of Captain Bligh away from Beery and give it to him. Laughton was grateful—to a point. "When I have a part like Captain Bligh or Father Barrett," he said, "I hate the man's guts so much that I overact. Parts like that make me physically sick."

While *Mutiny on the Bounty* was in preparation, Thalberg made two smaller films. His first 1935 release was an adaptation of a major Broadway hit, *Biography*. Thalberg had a curious connection to the play. Its star was Ina Claire, who had married Thalberg's friend John Gilbert in 1929 when Gilbert was on the rebound from Greta Garbo. Claire had flirted with movie stardom for three years, but she eventually tired of both Gilbert's moodiness and the filmmaking process. "I am through being stupid," she said on her way back to Broadway. She had an immediate triumph in S. N. Behrman's *Biography*, the story of a portrait painter famed for affairs with her subjects. Of course, Thalberg wanted to film the play. He was taken aback when Claire turned him down. He bought the play for Shearer, but she was unwilling to go straight from *The Barretts* to *Biography*. Unable to get a major M-G-M star, Thalberg settled on RKO's Ann Harding, who was an intelligent, convincing actress.

In order to get *Biography* passed by Joseph Breen, Thalberg made the painter whimsical rather than promiscuous, but he knew there was a limit to what he could cut. "Motion pictures have grown up—and so have the audiences," Thalberg told an interviewer. "Audiences are no longer made up of gullible babes, enthralled by the elementary. The man who puts gasoline in your car is a college man. You can't offer him a high-priced star and a glamorous publicity campaign and expect him to accept that as entertainment." *Biography of a Bachelor Girl* was clever and diverting, but Harding's lilting voice made critics long for Claire. "Ann Harding is a sedate substitute for Ina Claire," wrote Norbert Lusk, "[Claire] made the character of the bohemian artist anything but sedate." The film lost money. Was miscasting the problem or was the star just not big enough? Thalberg's next film would, in a way, answer that. He bought another Broadway play, and this time he had access to a major M-G-M star.

Joan Crawford was perceived by most of Hollywood, and not incorrectly, as Norma Shearer's rival. Since her comeback in the David Selznick production of *Dancing Lady*, Crawford had worked for all of Thalberg's former supervisors, playing parts that would hardly have been appropriate for Shearer, yet the perception remained. As might be expected, the two stars maintained separate salons. Shearer catered to Thalberg's need for rest after a very long work day. Crawford catered to her own need for cultural education, social advancement, and glamour. An evening at the home she shared with her fiancé, the Theatre Guild actor Franchot Tone, might include a recital by a visiting opera star or by Crawford herself. She had invited the Thalbergs to one of her soirees and been declined. "I was much too easily hurt," recalled Crawford. "If I asked people to dinner and they couldn't come, I'd wonder if they liked me." She was surprised, then, to receive an invitation to a Thalberg dinner, along with such regulars as the Charles Laughtons, the Clark Gables, and the Leslie Howards. "I don't know who was more frightened, Joan or me," recalled Shearer. "People said that I was inviting a friendly enemy to dinner. Joan proved them wrong by being a most delightful guest." Crawford was equally surprised when Thalberg cast her in his next film.

No More Ladies was the story of a wife who punishes her philandering husband by trapping him at a weekend party with his former conquests. Donald Ogden Stewart, who was becoming Thalberg's favorite screenwriter, made the film a pinwheel of brittle one-liners, bibulous supporting characters, and shallow emotions. "*No More Ladies* wasn't my picture," wrote Crawford. "It went strictly to Edna May Oliver as a highball-drinking grandmother, a grand dame who wore trains and said 'Scram.'" For all its deficiencies, the film made a healthy profit. It was not enough to satisfy Thalberg. Perhaps it was time for a break from the high art of Broadway. "To hell with art," said Thalberg. "This time I'm going to produce a picture that will make money."

Thalberg wanted Jeanette MacDonald for another production, but L. B. Mayer gave her to Hunt Stromberg, and she became a major star with *Naughty Marietta* and (here) *Rose Marie,* which was shot at Emerald Bay in Lake Tahoe. Mayer continued to withhold the biggest M-G-M stars from Thalberg's production unit, but MacDonald maintained the momentum Thalberg had given her. The films she made with Nelson Eddy would become (along with the Tarzan and Andy Hardy series) the studio's most lucrative. Photograph by Bert Lynch

Thalberg's first 1935 release was *Biography of a Bachelor Girl.* It was shot at Sky Forest in Lake Arrowhead. Thalberg borrowed Ann Harding from RKO-Radio Pictures to play the free-spirited artist. Photograph by Frank Tanner

In March 1935, Gable had not yet begun *Mutiny on the Bounty*, and Jean Harlow and Wallace Beery were finally available to Thalberg, so he mounted a three-star production and hired Tay Garnett, who was expert at directing stories set in exotic climes. For his source Thalberg chose *China Seas*, a minor novel with strong characters and conflicts. By the time a dozen writers had finished with it, it was not great Broadway art, but it was a real movie, a cinematic rollercoaster ride, a series of great scenes that both showcased its stars and tugged at the heart. "Thalberg had a very astute story mind, and I think he could have been a great writer," said assistant director Joe Newman. "When we had some trouble with the script on the set of *China Seas*, he would come down

to the set. Many times he would rewrite the scenes himself, right there on the set. Sometimes he'd dictate the changes so you could write them down. Sometimes he'd do it himself with a pencil." With a profit of more than $600,000, *China Seas* became the blockbuster hit that Thalberg needed to maintain his turf.

Five years earlier, Thalberg had made stars of Marie Dressler and Wallace Beery when the rest of Hollywood considered the two performers to be over-the-hill has-beens. With the same idea in mind, he signed the Marx Brothers to a personal contract. Their first few films for Paramount—*The Cocoanuts*, *Animal Crackers*, and *Monkey Business*—had been tremendously popular, but their trademarked anarchy had lost favor

Irving Thalberg and Norma Shearer were photographed at the Glendale train station on September 19, 1935.

by 1933's *Duck Soup*, and Paramount had washed its hands of them. Chico Marx was a regular at Thalberg's Thursday night bridge games, along with Constance Bennett, Sam Goldwyn, and Joseph Schenck (brother of Nick and head of the newly merged Twentieth Century-Fox). Before retiring to her bedroom, Shearer would serve refreshments to her guests. "You can imagine what kind of humor there was with Sam Goldwyn and a Marx brother at the same card table," she said. Thalberg was the only one laughing the night he won $14,000 from his guests.

The Marx Brothers numbered three—Harpo, Groucho, and Chico. (Zeppo, their straight man, had quit to become a talent agent.) Thalberg thought their act needed a new concept. "I don't agree with the principle of anything for a laugh," he said. "For my money, comedy scenes have to further the plot. It's more important to have a story that the audience is interested in than to have a laugh every other minute."

"So you didn't care for *Duck Soup*," said Groucho.

"Women didn't," replied Thalberg. "Your movies have strictly male appeal. Men like your comedy, but women don't. They don't understand your kind of humor. You have to start giving women what they want, a love interest, a romance they can become interested in." Groucho became more agreeable when Thalberg offered him and his brothers $7,500 a week and 15 percent of the gross. Thalberg also hired writers whom Groucho recommended, even though they included the most expensive in the business, George S. Kaufman—the co-author of *Dinner at Eight*, two Gershwin hits, and the Marx Brothers' stage success *Animal Crackers*. Kaufman did his time on the "million-dollar bench" outside Thalberg's office, waiting with the likes of Crawford and Garnett, and, once inside the office, found the producer a little condescending. Thalberg questioned Kaufman on plot points, machine-gun style.

"Did you bring me out here to write or to play Twenty Questions?" asked Kaufman.

"I brought you here—at considerable expense—to answer those and any other questions I might ask you," replied Thalberg.

"Very well, Mr. Thalberg. Ask away." A few conferences later, Kaufman saw Thalberg differently. "I feel like an idiot," Kaufman confessed to Groucho. "That man has never written a word, yet he can tell me exactly what to do with a story. I didn't know you had people like that out here."

Thalberg thought that the Marxes would be funnier if contrasted with an institution of rigid dignity. He was a patron of the Los Angeles Opera, so he decided that the Marx Brothers' M-G-M debut would be called *A Night at the Opera*. Groucho was not convinced that the gags in the script would work. "You can't sit in an office in Culver City and know what they're going to laugh at in St. Louis," he told Thalberg. "When we were on Broadway, we'd try a show out on the road for weeks before we'd bring it to New York."

"Why can't we do the same?" asked Thalberg.

"How can you try a picture out on the road?" demanded Groucho.

"You don't have to take the *picture* on the road, Groucho!" said Thalberg, who arranged for a tour of a five-scene digest of *A Night at the Opera*. "We made notes on every show," said Harpo. "When a line didn't get the laugh we expected, we changed it or threw it out." But this was not enough for Thalberg. He also put the film through a number of sneak previews, pruning bits here and there to improve its pace. The result was seen in November, when *A Night at the Opera* premiered in Hollywood. "Yesterday's audience at Grauman's Chinese Theatre was convulsed," reported the *Los Angeles Times*. "Their comedy bursts its shackles and spatters into magnificent fragments," wrote the *New York*

Times, "as the brothers, with the police and the opera management hard on their heels, transform Verdi into low buffoonery." *A Night at the Opera* was the nationwide hit that both Thalberg and the Marxes needed. He had restored their stardom and buttressed his own status at M-G-M. It remained for one more film to put him back on top.

Mutiny on the Bounty was becoming the epic Lloyd had envisioned. It required the purchase of two sailing vessels, the construction of a complete ship interior, and the ferrying of all three to Santa Catalina Island, where the studio also built replicas of Portsmouth Harbor and a Tahitian village, as well as a soundstage and barracks to house cast and crew for two months. Albert Lewin was Thalberg's associate producer—with credit, no less. At times, Lewin thought he was headed for a nervous breakdown or a heart attack, what with quarrels between Gable and Laughton and seagoing accidents, one of which drowned a crew member. Lewin complained to Thalberg of palpitations. "Hell, those are nothing," replied Thalberg. "I get those all the time."

Thalberg's health remained constant during this period, but Shearer monitored him closely. He kept bottles of medicine and vitamins in his desk drawers, and carried nitroglycerine tablets in his vest pocket. An assistant stayed nearby with dried fruit, chocolate bars, Coca Cola, and other mild stimulants. Thalberg's only real stimulant was making a movie, and he spared himself little. Even though Shearer was pregnant with their second child, she often stayed up past midnight waiting for him to come home. "His head would vibrate at night," recalled Frances Goldwyn. "You could feel his heart throbbing in the palms of his hands. In spite of all that, he was handsome in a unique way."

Thalberg looked handsome and healthy when he accepted the Academy Award for Best Picture of 1935, won by *Mutiny on the Bounty*. Of equal importance were the film's grosses of $4.5 million. Thalberg had correctly gauged the public's willingness to sit through a long, brutal film that was almost unrelieved by love interest. "People are fascinated by cruelty," he told a skeptical Nick Schenck at one point. When Schenck had first seen the film in New York, he had predicted a disastrous flop. "Tell Thalberg it's the worst picture M-G-M has ever made!" he had said. With Captain Bligh and Fletcher Christian wowing audiences all over the world, Thalberg was vindicated. He had made three of the biggest, most talked about, and most profitable films of the year, so he set his sights even higher.

It was time for another Shearer film. She had given birth to a baby girl on June 14. The Thalbergs named her Katharine (after Katharine Cornell). Shearer began to prepare for her return to the screen. Thalberg had earlier announced *Pride and Prejudice* and *Marie Antoinette* as vehicles for her. When he asked her what she wanted, she replied offhandedly: "I think I'd like to do Juliet." Thalberg had already approached Cornell about reprising her stage success in *Romeo and Juliet*. "I am interested only in the stage," she said. "It is the medium best suited for whatever talent I may possess." Thalberg laughed at Shearer when she told him she wanted to play Shakespeare. She was a pregnant thirty-two year old. Juliet was supposed to be fourteen. Then he thought about it and spent the next month convincing Mayer and Schenck to back an M-G-M production of *Romeo and Juliet*.

No More Ladies was distinguished by an upstaging contest between Joan Crawford's artificial eyelashes and Edna May Oliver's rubber face.

Jean Harlow, Clark Gable, and Wallace Beery all owed their stardom to Thalberg. In a sudden shift from drawing-room comedies to rowdy crowd-pleasers, he co-starred them in the adventure film *China Seas*. Photograph by Virgil Apger

The scenes between Harlow and Beery in *China Seas* bristled with hostility. Beery was notoriously rude to coworkers and Harlow was anxious about her big dramatic scenes. Thalberg had perfected a formula for Harlow, a blend of innocence and sensuality that made the "Platinum Blonde" as lovable as she was desirable. His formula for Beery was to temper meanness with sloppy sentimentality. Photograph by Virgil Apger

Harpo, Chico, and Groucho Marx posed for this publicity shot outside the M-G-M gates before Thalberg had decided what to do with them. Photograph by Clarence Bull

Walter Woolf King was one of numerous Marx Brothers victims in *A Night at the Opera.*

Thalberg posed with the Marx Brothers during a story conference.

The radically different acting styles of Charles Laughton and Clark Gable gave *Mutiny on the Bounty* a special tension. The two actors had a long period of adjustment. Gable accused Laughton of upstaging him. Laughton looked Gable up and down as if he were a juicy steak. According to Anita Loos, Thalberg liked this interpretation. "The rivalry between Bligh and Christian was so bitter," said Loos, "that it could only be based on mutual fascination."

Opposite: *Mutiny on the Bounty* was Thalberg's third million-dollar production in 1935. This scene of Clark Gable and Franchot Tone leaving Eddie Quillan on Tahiti was one of many complex sequences shot on Catalina Island.

Charles Laughton found Captain William Bligh painful to portray. Photograph by Clarence Bull

Clark Gable, seen here with Mamo Clark, did not believe he had given a great performance in *Mutiny on the Bounty*. "After the picture was finished," he said later, "I went to South America on a ten-week holiday, and while I was there they previewed *Mutiny*. I got a cablegram from Thalberg: 'The movie is wonderful. We're proud of it. You'll like yourself in it.' I had to believe Irving because he was a guy you could believe. He didn't kid himself or anybody else."

During filming of the balcony scene in *Romeo and Juliet,* Thalberg stood in the shadows of Stage 15 and watched in rapt attention as Norma Shearer recited Shakespeare's couplets to Leslie Howard. Photograph by William Grimes

1936

In January 1936, Irving Thalberg's bungalow was humming with projects. *The Prisoner of Zenda, Knights of the Round Table,* and *Goodbye, Mr. Chips* had been announced as upcoming productions. *Peace and Quiet, Camille,* and *Maytime* were in preparation. *Romeo and Juliet* and *The Good Earth* were in production. A Jean Harlow film called *Riffraff* was premiering on January 3. To have two films of this magnitude on track would be enough for any Hollywood producer. To have nine was extraordinary, especially for an individual with health concerns.

Riffraff was an experiment. Thalberg wanted to see if Harlow could repeat the intensity of her dramatic scenes in *China Seas.* This film was also introducing the "New Jean Harlow." Since the enforcement of the Production Code, scarlet floozies had been chased off the screen. *China Seas* had encountered resistance from Joseph Breen because of Harlow's uncertain profession. Thalberg decided to soften her image. Her bleach-damaged hair was covered with a "brownette" wig, and she was cast as a poor but honest cannery worker. The "Platinum Blonde" was gone. "I always hated my hair," said Harlow, "not only because it limited me as an actress, but also because it limited me as a person. It made me look hard and spectacular. I had to live up to that platinum personality." As Thalberg knew from his dinner parties, the real Harlow was gentle and soft-spoken; that was the person he put in *Riffraff.*

"Occasionally Thalberg would write a memo, but he was not at his best with the written word," recalled David Lewis, associate producer on *Riffraff.* "Sometimes he would even try to write a scene. But while the idea was generally excellent, the delivery was invariably disastrous. He wanted to be a writer more than anything in the world, but he just didn't have the flair for writing, and he was too stubborn to admit it. But the way his mind moved and the depth of his character understanding was magnificent." Albert Lewin recalled Thalberg's self-consciousness about his prose. "Irving always wanted me to correct the speeches he gave at luncheons and civic affairs," said Lewin. "He would give them to me and wait for me to comment. He was more widely read than some college professors I knew, but like many people with little formal education, he overestimated the value of higher education."

Thalberg was impressed by academics. He invited Cornell University's William Strunk Jr., the renowned Shakespeare expert, to help adapt William Shakespeare's *Romeo and Juliet.* Thalberg felt that a scholarly imprimatur was necessary, but there was another reason for courting prestige. He wanted to strengthen his position. Neither Louis B. Mayer nor Nick Schenck wanted to make *Romeo and Juliet.* Schenck did not mince words. "It's a silly idea, Irving," said Schenck.

"It's the greatest love story ever told," was Thalberg's response to naysayers. "It's a work of art." When he declared his intention to star his wife as Juliet in the first authentic Shakespeare film, he encountered more opposition.

"How can a thirtyish wife play a fourteen-year-old virgin?" Kate Corbaley asked story editor Sam Marx.

"I believe Norma can play anything—and do it better than anyone else," Thalberg told Marx, and then sought support for his heartfelt project. He approached director George Cukor (who said yes), Clark Gable (who said no), forty-two-year-old Leslie Howard (who said maybe), and publicity director Howard Dietz (who promised to sell America on the Bard). To seal the deal, Thalberg promised not to spend more than $800,000 on *Romeo and Juliet*. When Schenck gave Thalberg the go-ahead, Mayer snidely predicted another "prestige picture." Thalberg was determined to prove him wrong. He prepared the most carefully researched, expertly advised, thoroughly rehearsed, beautifully designed, lavishly mounted, magnificently photographed, skillfully edited film of the year. Its trappings were dazzling: antiques purchased in Italy; two costume designers (Gilbert Adrian and Oliver Messel); a thousand individually executed Renaissance costumes; the largest Capulet ballroom and garden ever built; four still photographers (William Grimes, Clarence Bull, Ted Allan, and George Hurrell); dances choreographed by Agnes de Mille; dramatic coaching by Constance Collier, Mrs. Frances Robinson Duff, and Margaret Carrington; Basil Rathbone as Tybalt; John Barrymore as Mercutio; and Leslie Howard as Romeo. All this for $800,000? Thalberg was so busy with his other productions that he lost track of the cost, and no one at Loew's, Inc., called him to account.

His other productions were as big as—or bigger—than *Romeo and Juliet*. *The Good Earth* required the construction of two full-size Chinese farming villages, one outside Culver City and one in the San Fernando Valley. *Camille* had English novelist James Hilton and Thalberg stalwart Frances Marion on its script, and

Greta Garbo as the fabled courtesan Marguerite Gautier. Then Thalberg found the script unusable and hired playwright Zoë Akins to write an entirely new one. Transforming *Maytime* from a 1917 operetta to a 1937 film required the services of its veteran composer, Sigmund Romberg, as well as those of Edmund Goulding. Thalberg decided that *Maytime* should be M-G-M's first feature shot entirely in Technicolor, which instantly upped its budget 50 percent; the super-popular team of Jeanette MacDonald and Nelson Eddy was expected to justify the cost. Similarly, the renewed drawing power of the Marx Brothers was expected to pay for the eighteen scripts that turned *Peace and Quiet* into *A Day at the Races*. Thalberg spent sixteen-hour days in his oak-paneled bungalow juggling these facts, making these decisions, and motivating these artists. What motivated him was the thrill of filmmaking.

Thalberg would have preferred to seclude himself in a creative cloister, but Hollywood politics demanded his presence at social affairs. In the first three quarters of 1936, he clocked more than forty events. These included the Ballet Russe opening, January 24; the Jewish Center Association banquet, February 10; Charles Chaplin's *Modern Times* premiere, February 12; Joan Crawford's Leopold Stokowski party, March 1; a Museum of Modern Art Film Library meeting, March 27; the Actors' Fund Benefit Ball, July 1; and the opening of Tallulah Bankhead's *Reflected Glory* on August 10. He was a guest speaker at Carl Laemmle's thirtieth-anniversary party on February 27, and he was toastmaster at Laemmle's sudden farewell party on April 22 (after the Laemmles had lost bankrupt Universal). Thalberg was a sponsor of Jewish refugees from Hitler's Germany, as well as a silent underwriter of Rabbi Edgar F. Magnin's magnificent Wilshire Boulevard Temple.

Not so silent was Thalberg's opposition to the Hollywood labor movement. After twelve years of running the most successful company in America's sixth-largest industry, he regarded the dialogue between labor and management as a prelude to revolution. He spent a good deal of time and even more energy in the spring of 1936 squelching the Screen Writers Guild (SWG). "These writers are living like kings," he told Salka Viertel. "Why on earth would they want to join a union, like coal miners or plumbers?" His rhetorical question fell on deaf and resentful ears. Most writers were eking out a living, helped not a whit by Thalberg's practices: they were lent from studio to studio without consent, made to write on speculation, suspended or laid off without written notice, denied screen credit according to their contribution, and made to work simultaneously on the same material without being informed of this by the producer. Writers who complained about any of these practices were blacklisted.

The conflict came to a head in early May, when the SWG threatened to go on strike. Thalberg saw a Communist conspiracy behind it. He called the writers to an emergency meeting and declared that he was not going to acknowledge the guild or its demands. He had spent twelve years building the best writing staff in the world. He had compensated them handsomely, treated them with loyalty and consideration, kept them on salary between assignments, and given them a livelihood year after year. Now the same favored employees were contemplating action that would harm not only themselves but also the thousands of studio employees who had families to support. "Understand this," he said in a cold, peremptory tone. "If you are foolhardy enough to proceed with this strike, I shall close down the entire plant, without a single exception." The room was silent as Thalberg started to walk out. Then he stopped and turned to the writers. "Make no mistake," he said quietly. "I mean precisely what I say. I shall close this studio, lock the gates, and there will be an end to Metro-Goldwyn-Mayer productions. And it will be you—the writers—who will have done it." The strike did not take place, but both sides walked away unsatisfied, bitter, and exhausted. It was no wonder, then, that Thalberg began to exhibit signs of fatigue.

The Good Earth director Sidney Franklin would often see Thalberg wolf down his dinner before a preview. "Irving, you'll kill yourself some day doing this," said Franklin. Thalberg's excuse was that he had to eat when he could. He ate cornflakes for dinner because it was easy to carry the bowl to his screening room. In the late spring, when Frances Marion came to see Thalberg for the first time in several months, she saw a change. "Irving looked

On March 5, 1936, Irving Thalberg collected an Academy Award when *Mutiny on the Bounty* was voted Best Picture of 1935; shown with him here is presenter Frank Capra.

so spent I could hardly conceal my alarm," wrote Marion. "He was underweight again and he walked with his head slightly tilted to one side, as if he were too frail to hold his head erect." Shearer confided to her friend Merle Oberon that Thalberg often had to lie down at the end of a work day because of the throbbing in his head. His stillness and lack of color frightened her. Adela Rogers St. Johns saw Thalberg in the summer of 1936. "He looked like a little figure made of white ashes," she recalled. "He had that kind of frailness that you see in young people before death." Yet Thalberg pushed on day after day. He tired in the late afternoon, but then, renewed by a nap, he continued into the evening. No one succeeded in slowing him. "Irving did nothing but work," recalled Anita Loos. "He was warned—numerous times. Do you know what he said? He said he'd rather die than stop working." In jest or not, death was a theme in the Thalberg bungalow. *Romeo and Juliet*; *The Good Earth*; *Camille, Goodbye, Mr. Chips*; and *Marie Antoinette* all lost characters to premature death.

Thalberg was not known for religious or even philosophical convictions. "Entertainment is Irving's god," said Charles MacArthur. Thalberg was a member of the B'nai B'rith Congregation, but unlike Mayer he was not given to religious talk. Thalberg was as guarded as Mayer was sententious. Thalberg reserved his quiet devotion for filmmaking. The only other love objects in his self-contained world were his mother (who was still resentful that he had moved away with his wife five years earlier), Norma Shearer, and his two children. He spent every morning playing with his children, and he often brought Irving Jr. to the studio with him. He catered to the boy but did not spoil him. When Irving Jr. asked for the beautiful model of the HMS *Bounty* that he saw in the bungalow, Irving Sr. told him he had to earn it by proving that he could swim across the pool at home. There was a bittersweet quality about Thalberg's attention to his children. He expected them to become the next generation of film artists but had doubts about his own longevity. After Katharine's birth, he had a burst of hope. A year later, he was trying not to think about death.

John Gilbert, perhaps the biggest star Thalberg ever created, died of alcoholism on January 9, 1936. He was thirty-eight years old. Thalberg was embarrassed by Marlene Dietrich's display of emotion at Gilbert's funeral. She was, after all, not his widow; he had been divorced by Virginia Bruce, who was present. But Dietrich moaned, staggered, and fell in the aisle (much as Pola Negri had done at Rudolph Valentino's funeral ten years earlier). It was a true "Hollywood funeral." A few days later, Shearer was enacting the *Romeo and Juliet* farewell scene with Leslie Howard. She involuntarily burst into tears. "Some of the tears I shed in *Romeo and Juliet* were for your wonderful father," she later told Gilbert's daughter Leatrice. (Shearer had made her first M-G-M film with Gilbert and had played the *Romeo and Juliet* balcony scene with him in *The Hollywood Revue of 1929*.) Honest emotion or not, Thalberg felt it was too much, and he told her so. "It's beautiful," he said, "but if the parting were done, in a sense, with a smile, it would be more . . . more *poignant*." Perhaps he was trying to prepare her.

One summer afternoon, Thalberg was sitting by his pool, studying a script with Al Lewin. "I was sitting in the sunshine," Lewin recalled. "Irving was in the shade of an umbrella. Norma was in the pool with Katharine, teaching her to dog paddle. Irving Jr. was practicing diving. Breakers were crashing on the beach a few feet away. It was an idyllic scene, to say the least." Lewin suddenly found himself looking at Thalberg in the abstract. "Irving," said Lewin.

"What?"

"If I were you, I'd be worried."

"About this dialogue?"

"No, no."

"About what, then?"

"I was looking at you and it occurred to me," said Lewin. "You've just turned thirty-seven, and you've got everything that a man could want. You've got millions. You're a captain of industry. You have a lovely, talented wife, and two beautiful, healthy children." Thalberg nodded. "The gods hate people like you. They're probably hiding behind that wall with a great big bat."

"You're right," Thalberg laughed. "You're absolutely right." He glanced at the wall, which belonged to his neighbor Douglas Fairbanks. Then he chuckled and went back to the script in his hand.

In early September, *Camille* was under way. Thalberg was happy with what he had seen of Garbo's performance. "I think we have caught Garbo as she should be caught," he said. "She will be the most memorable Camille of our time." Sam Marx asked Thalberg how the production was going. "If only they were all like this," answered Thalberg, referring to *Maytime*, which had started shooting with an incomplete script. "Goulding would write it every night at home," recalled Joe Newman, "and I would take it over to Thalberg's home in Santa Monica." The mood on the *Camille* set changed as a heat wave sat on Los Angeles and Garbo began to feel unwell. When she saw Thalberg standing on the sidelines of the set, she told the assistant director to speak to him. She did not like being watched. "I've been put off better sets than this one," said Thalberg on his way out, but no one could remember it happening before. Thalberg was more concerned with *Romeo and Juliet*, which was going into a special limited-engagement release. The reviews had hurt.

"I hesitate to call the picture great in the transcendental sense," wrote the *Los Angeles Times* critic, "yet there is fierce magic in it." The *New York Herald Tribune* wrote: "Miss Shearer is remarkably good. She is inclined to coyness at the start, but from the balcony scene on

she plays with simple intensity and profound assurance. In her most ambitious role she does the finest acting of her career." The *New York Times* wrote: "Metro the magnificent has loosed its technical magic upon Will Shakespeare and has fashioned for his *Romeo and Juliet* a jeweled setting in which the deep beauty of his romance glows and sparkles and gleams with breathless radiance. It is a dignified, sensitive and entirely admirable Shakespearean—not Hollywoodian—production." If Thalberg found this ambiguous, he must have found *Time* magazine's review insulting. It completely ignored Shearer's performance and gave him a backhanded compliment. "To avoid any possible gaffes in this production, Metro-Goldwyn-Mayer's star producer Irving Thalberg did everything except recall Shakespeare from the grave."

For the first time in his career, Thalberg had worn his heart on his sleeve. The man who never expressed emotion had tried to express it on film and for a film, and he had been rejected. *Romeo and Juliet*, the production that he wanted to succeed more than any other, was turning out to be a "qualified success." It was not the "prestige picture" that Mayer had predicted, but neither was it the blockbuster that it needed to be. Thalberg had spent an irretrievable $2.06 million on *Romeo and Juliet*. The film was doing well in the big cities, but to show a profit it would have to do as well as *Ben-Hur* and *The Big Parade* combined, and that was impossible. For the first time, Thalberg took a film's failure personally. "We were faithful to Shakespeare," he told Marx, "and I still hope the public will appreciate it." On September 4, after Thalberg read the first exhibitor reports, he was more frank with publicist Ralph Wheelwright. "I am bitterly disappointed," he said. To his associates he looked depressed.

He was also tired, but he nonetheless took on another project. The *Everyman Pageant* was a theatrical presentation of a medieval play for the benefit of Jewish refugees. Thalberg's participation required him to sit at the Hollywood Bowl in the cool evening air after working all day at M-G-M in the heat wave. The opening night would be September 10, three days after Labor Day. On Friday, September 4, Thalberg and Shearer were preparing for a Labor Day holiday trip to the Del Monte Lodge, where they celebrated their wedding anniversary every year. Joining them at the lodge were Harpo Marx, the Mervyn LeRoys, the Sam Marxes, the Robert Z. Leonards, the Jack Conways, the Sam Woods, and the Chico Marxes. Before they drove to their chartered plane at the Municipal Airport, two odd things occurred.

At five P.M. Shearer was playing several scenes from *Romeo and Juliet* on Louella Parsons's CBS radio show *Hollywood Hotel.* After she finished her last scene, she thought she heard someone—or something—speak to her. Quite clearly, the voice said: "You will never act again." At roughly the same time, David Lewis was in Thalberg's office, conferring with him about *Camille.* "We were waiting for Norma to come back from the radio station with Louella Parsons," recalled Lewis. "While we were talking, I said something about 'ten years from now.'"

"I'm not going to be here ten years from now," said Thalberg.

"Irving!" exclaimed Lewis.

"I might not be here ten days from now," Thalberg said matter-of-factly. Thalberg gave Lewis a quizzical look, and then realized that he had shocked him. "Pay no attention to my nonsense," said Thalberg.

Unlike Labor Day of 1932, when Paul Bern had died, this weekend truly was a holiday for M-G-M employees. Albert Lewin, David Lewis, and all the other producers who had not been invited to join Thalberg spent their coveted time off trying not to think about budgets or schedules. When Thalberg came back from the Monterey peninsula on Monday, he had a cold;

he had reportedly caught a chill from an ocean breeze while playing cards with Chico Marx and some others on the terrace of the Del Monte Lodge. Shearer tried unsuccessfully to keep him home. Lewis got a strange call from her on Tuesday. "Would you be willing to fly east with Irving?" she asked. "It's necessary." Thalberg needed to see a specialist. "He wants someone to fly with him. I know you fly. Nobody else I know does."

Lewis and Franklin noticed that Thalberg was away from the office all week. On Friday, Thalberg was still absent, but Lewis told Franklin not to worry; Norma had called to say that there would be no emergency flight. Irving was better. On Sunday, September 13, most of the studio's three thousand employees attended the annual studio picnic. The Thalbergs did not. Eddie Mannix read a message over the public address system on the picnic grounds: "Only illness prevents me from being with you today. Best wishes, Irving Thalberg." Mannix, Lewin, and several others had stopped by Thalberg's home on the way to the picnic; they were unusually quiet all day. On Sunday night, Mayer's cronies were surprised when he canceled plans to meet them at the Trocadero nightclub. He spent the evening at his home, speaking to no one. He would later tell intimates that he passed the night asking himself what had gone wrong between him and Thalberg since the "Mission Road days."

Early on the morning of Monday, September 14, Mayer gathered his associates in his office and quietly informed them that Irving Thalberg was gravely ill with pneumonia. He had stopped by the Thalberg home on his way to the studio and learned that Thalberg had rallied around dawn. He was now under an oxygen tent. He was not able to recognize anyone or to speak. No one was sure how he had fallen so ill so quickly. He had only been diagnosed with strep throat on Friday. There was nothing to do but wait. Mayer's office fell silent. His associates sat in plush chairs, looking out at the stages Thalberg had helped to build. At 10:30 the telephone rang in the outer office. A buzzer sounded on Mayer's desk. He answered his telephone, then hung up without speaking. He rose from his desk and told his men: "Irving is dead."

Office by office, stage by stage, the news arrived at M-G-M. Filming stopped on *Maytime*, *Camille*, and *Born to Dance*. Director Sam Wood walked slowly onto the set of *A Day at the Races*. His face was streaked with tears. "The little brown fellow just died," he blurted. Cries of disbelief were heard. Lights were doused. Work was suspended. "The studio was absolutely devastated, shocked," said Lewis. "No matter what had happened at the highest levels, Thalberg was respected and loved by the ordinary people at the studio. In many ways he had been the symbol of M-G-M's greatness. Enormous headlines, not only in Los Angeles but also all across the country, screamed: "THALBERG DEAD!"

Basil Rathbone had recently costarred on Broadway with Katharine Cornell in *Romeo and Juliet*. When Thalberg cast his Romeo, Rathbone was not considered. The highest-paid supporting actor in Hollywood had to content himself with Tybalt. Photograph by Ted Allan

While waiting for his scenes to be shot, Rathbone did some shooting of his own. He used a 35mm Leica camera to make this snapshot of Clark Gable, who was filming *San Francisco* on an adjoining sound-stage. Thalberg had sponsored *San Francisco* but turned it over to another producer when it began to compete with *Romeo and Juliet* for his attention. Photograph by Basil Rathbone. Courtesy of Michael Epstein, hurrellphotos.com

Cameraman William Daniels made *Romeo and Juliet* perhaps the most beautifully lit film of the entire black-and-white era. Cedric Gibbons designed the Capulet garden set so there would be "a physical obstacle for Romeo to overcome" on his way to Juliet's balcony. Forty-six-year-old Leslie Howard (seen here) managed to scale the Capulet walls without aid of a double; few first-nighters complained that he was thirty years too old to play Romeo. Photograph by William Grimes

Rathbone shot this artfully composed image in the courtyard where he was fighting a duel with John Barrymore. Photograph by Basil Rathbone. Courtesy of Michael Epstein, hurrellphotos.com

The bed in *Romeo and Juliet* was a far cry from the silken divans of Shearer's earlier films, but the PCA's Joseph Breen was still vigilant. He warned Thalberg to avoid filming any "action of Romeo and Juliet lying on the bed, fondling one another in a horizontal position, and pulling one another down." Lighting by William Daniels; photograph by William Grimes

While directing *The Good Earth*, Sidney Franklin posed with a Chinese water buffalo who could act.

Thalberg's production of *The Good Earth* mandated the construction of two Chinese farming communities, complete with wheat fields, rice fields, and real farmhouses, imported in sections from China.

Thalberg held that for a film to be great, it must have one great sequence. He invested *The Good Earth* with four show-stopping sequences. The fourth of these showed a battle between farmers and crop-devouring insects. Laurence Stallings wrote: "I have witnessed queues of fans standing outside theaters in New York, Paris, and London, just to see a swarm of locusts descend from heaven in a cloud of horror."

Thalberg liked George Cukor's handling of Garbo and Lenore Ulric in *Camille*'s early scenes.

"George, she's awfully good," Thalberg said of Garbo. "I don't think I've ever seen her so good."

"But Irving, she's just sitting in an opera box," said Cukor.

"She's relaxed," said Thalberg. "She's open. She seems unguarded for once."

Photograph by William Grimes

Opposite: When Garbo acted a coughing spell for *Camille* on August 20, she was beginning to feel unwell herself. Even so, she was giving a luminous performance as Marguerite Gautier. Photograph by William Grimes

The Thalberg family sat for a series of portraits by a talented but uncredited photographer in April 1936. At the time, baby Katharine was not yet a year old. Irving Jr. was nearing six. Thalberg was thirty-six, and Shearer was thirty-three.

Opposite: In early August 1936, Thalberg and Shearer sailed to Catalina Island on Baron Long's yacht *Norab*. Relaxed weekends were rare in the last months of Thalberg's life.

After Irving Thalberg's death, his projects were taken from his assistants and reworked by new producers. Bernard Hyman shot numerous new scenes for *Camille*. They were discarded when an executive realized that Thalberg's version was better. This portrait of Greta Garbo as Marguerite Gautier was made on November 23, 1936, a day after she had finished shooting (and reshooting) *Camille*. The film did well, and Garbo was honored with an Academy Award nomination, the New York Film Critics Award, and the "Littris et Artibus" decoration from King Gustav of Sweden. More importantly, *Camille* came to be regarded as her greatest film and the definitive interpretation of Dumas *fils*'s tragic heroine. Thirty years later, the reclusive star asked the Museum of Modern Art to screen it privately for her and a friend, remarking afterward: "It holds up well, doesn't it?"

THE LEGACY

For thirteen years, there had never been a question as to what Irving Thalberg wanted. Suddenly an entire corporation was trying to do what he would have wanted. It began with his funeral. It was not a "Hollywood funeral" because he would not have wanted his family to endure anything vulgar. The service was conducted by Rabbi Edgar F. Magnin, who was the spiritual leader of the Los Angeles Jewish community and a Thalberg confidant. Magnin emphasized Thalberg's modesty, both as a producer and as a philanthropist. "The world knows his accomplishments," said Rabbi Magnin, "but few know the real part he took in community life. You could always call on Irving. He would listen." After the eulogy, one studio executive whispered to another: "They won't miss him today or tomorrow or six months from now or a year from now. But two years from now they'll begin to feel the squeeze." He was wrong. The squeeze was felt as soon as M-G-M tallied Thalberg's projects.

The Good Earth was nearly completed. Mayer suggested that a title card be inserted after Leo the Lion and before the credits. It read: "To the Memory of Irving Grant Thalberg We Dedicate this Picture, His Last Great Achievement." *The Good Earth* was voted one of 1937's Ten Best by the *New York Times* and several trade papers. Box office was another matter. Thalberg's last achievement was also his last prestige picture, gaining great reviews and losing half a million dollars.

Marie Antoinette; *Goodbye, Mr. Chips*; and *Pride and Prejudice* were still being written. All three were shelved, along with early drafts of Henryk Sienkiewicz's *Quo Vadis*, Anthony Hope's *The Prisoner of Zenda*, and Mary Roberts Rinehart's *Tish*. George Cukor's *Camille* had nearly finished shooting. Sam Wood's *A Day at the Races* had just started. Edmund Goulding's *Maytime* was not doing well; he was still writing it as he went along. "These are Irving's last pictures," Eddie Mannix told Bernard Hyman. "If anything can be done to make them better, do it, no matter what the expense." *A Day at the Races* was assigned to Lawrence Weingarten, who made sure that writers and director alike respected the template Thalberg had created in *A Night at the Opera*. The result was a somewhat homogenized version of the Marx Brothers' humor, but the film grossed $5 million, more than any of their other films. Goulding was yanked off *Maytime*, and Hunt Stromberg took over, creating another hit. It was not the saucy Technicolor film that Thalberg had envisioned, but its craftsmanship and sincerity honored his principles.

The most important of Thalberg's unfinished projects was *Camille*. Bernard Hyman took it away from Thalberg's protégé David Lewis. Hyman was not qualified to take control of the delicately shaded opus, but like most Hollywood producers he was too proud to admit it. He had a new opening written for the film,

The Good Earth was released in January 1937, four months after Thalberg's death. It starred the Jewish-American Paul Muni and the Viennese Luise Rainer as Chinese farmers. Thalberg hoped that the humanity of their story would transcend time, place, and nationality. Like many other classic films, *The Good Earth* lost money on its initial release but made it up in reissues, television, 16mm rentals, video, cable TV, and DVD. It is one of Thalberg's most honored films.

and before he was done he had spent $100,000 in new scenes. Trying to improve on Thalberg was an exercise in foolishness. When the film was previewed, the audience laughed at it and showed no sympathy for the Lady of the Camellias. Lewis, who was still at the studio, went over Hyman's head and asked Mannix for help. The tough executive was also fair. He told Hyman to return the film to its original form. It became Garbo's signature film.

Thalberg had championed Garbo, but his primary interest was in Norma Shearer. Passing her days in seclusion, she felt an incalculable loss. She was grieving for Thalberg and grieving for the guidance he could no longer give her. After the premiere of *Romeo and Juliet*, Mayer sent word to her, telling her that he would proceed with *Marie Antoinette* whenever she was ready. The mammoth project consumed her energies for nearly a year, and she had misgivings about its integrity when Mayer summarily replaced Sidney Franklin with "One-Take" Woody Van Dyke. Fortunately she was able to exert sufficient pressure on producer Hunt Stromberg to keep the project within calling distance of Thalberg's original concept. "And so *Marie Antoinette* was made," she wrote Franklin in 1955. "I was going to say without you or Irving, but as far as I was concerned, you were both there, tapping me on the shoulder." Shearer worked at M-G-M until she was no longer offered prestige projects. Without Thalberg to guide her and fight for her, she saw no reason to continue. She retired in 1942. The films that Thalberg made for her colleagues were rediscovered and reappraised in the early 1970s, but Shearer's early films were passed over. Only in the 1990s were films such as *Lady of the Night, The Divorcee*, and *A Free Soul* recognized for the achievements they were. Irving Thalberg's legacy began to shine more brightly.

TO THE MEMORY OF
IRVING GRANT THALBERG
WE DEDICATE THIS PICTURE
HIS LAST GREAT ACHIEVEMENT

The Good Earth was the first M-G-M film to bear Thalberg's name. Louis B. Mayer added this preface to the film's opening titles. "Everybody felt distracted at Irving's death," said Albert Lewin. "It was kind of an earthquake, not only for Metro, but for the industry. He had been universally loved and admired. The entire industry was shaken by his death."

At the premiere of *Marie Antoinette*, Shearer received spontaneous applause for several scenes, including this one, in which she manages a wan smile on her way to the guillotine. It was her night of triumph, but she made sure that the name of Irving Thalberg was spoken numerous times.

Opposite: The project to which Thalberg had devoted the most time and energy before he died was an adaptation of Stefan Zweig's *Marie Antoinette*. It was posthumously produced by Hunt Stromberg and directed by W. S. Van Dyke II. Years earlier Shearer had told Thalberg that Marie Antoinette would be the part of a lifetime. Her stylized, powerful performance was an impressive achievement in a field dominated by Greta Garbo, Katharine Hepburn, and Bette Davis. Photograph by Laszlo Willinger

Shearer's second film after Thalberg's passing was a project of which he would have undoubtedly approved, an adaptation of Robert Sherwood's *Idiot's Delight*, the Broadway hit starring Alfred Lunt and Lynn Fontanne. She played Irene as glamour incarnate. Photograph by Laszlo Willinger

Robert Ingersoll Aitken sculpted the first version of the Irving Thalberg Award
for the Academy of Motion Picture Arts and Sciences. This 1941 photograph
shows Norma Shearer with the artist's proof of her late husband.

EPILOGUE

Our visit to Irving Thalberg's M-G-M ends in 1939. This was the year in which his contract with Metro-Goldwyn-Mayer would have lapsed. Had he lived, he would have left the studio he cofounded fifteen years earlier and founded his own company, the I. G. Thalberg Corporation. He would have taken the artists under personal contract to him—Norma Shearer, Charles Laughton, the Marx Brothers, Donald Ogden Stewart, David Lewis, and Albert Lewin among them—and made films for release by United Artists. Among the properties he might have adapted are Jane Austen's *Pride and Prejudice*, Henryk Sienkiewicz's *Quo Vadis*, Anthony Hope's *The Prisoner of Zenda*, Franz Werfel's *The Forty Days of Musa Dagh*, and Sinclair Lewis's *It Can't Happen Here*. Many of these were filmed by other producers, and were done well. We can only speculate what Thalberg would have brought to them. What facet would he have polished to make the story sparkle more brightly? What aspect would he have sharpened to etch a character more deeply? What star would he have cast to create a classic performance? The answers to these questions can be found, perhaps, in the films made by his former colleagues.

While it is unfair to describe Hunt Stromberg, David Lewis, or Albert Lewin as Thalberg disciples, the films they produced after his death do reflect his goal of synthesizing theater and cinema. There is no way to know what Thalberg would have thought of Stromberg's *The Women*, Lewis's *Dark Victory*, or Lewin's *The Picture of Dorian Gray*. He may not have thought them worth filming. *Dark Victory*, for example, was bought by David Selznick while Thalberg was living. Only later did it find its way to Warner Bros., where Lewis produced it. Would Thalberg have rewritten major portions of *The Women*? He might have added men to its cast, as did the 1956 remake. He might have made Norma Shearer's Mary Haines less noble and more combative. He might have sent her and Joan Crawford back to the soundstage for retakes. He might have cast it differently. After all, *The Women* was bought by M-G-M as a vehicle for Jean Harlow, not Joan Crawford. Visualize Harlow (in her *Red-Headed Woman* mode) as Crystal, Crawford (in her *Mildred Pierce* mode) as Mary, and Shearer (in her *Private Lives* mode) as the wacky, nasty Sylvia. If Thalberg had filmed *The Picture of Dorian Gray*, he might have emphasized the bisexual elements of Oscar Wilde's story, much as he had recommended this to the writers of *Queen Christina*.

What about the stars Thalberg groomed? Imagine where he might have taken Harlow's career. He might have brought her to his new company and made her the foremost comic star of the 1940s, precluding the ascendance of Lucille Ball. He might have borrowed Clark Gable and Carole Lombard for his own version of *My Favorite Wife*. He was planning, in fact, to remake *The Hunchback of Notre Dame* with Charles Laughton. He probably would have taken the Marx Brothers somewhere other than the Big Store, the Circus, or the Wild West. Their film careers would have lasted longer, jointly and singly, if Thalberg had guided them.

Thalberg could have prevented the sad things that M-G-M did to its female stars in the early 1940s. Jeanette MacDonald's career began to slide in 1937, when she inadvertently offended Louis B. Mayer. (She went to Nick Schenck about a problem instead of going to Mayer.) The vogue for operettas was obviously waning, but she need not have bowed out in her prime simply because Mayer wanted to punish her. Myrna Loy's career ran out of steam because M-G-M put her in too many *Thin Man* sequels (and copies). To get a serious part, she had to go to Twentieth Century-Fox for *The Rains Came*. Thalberg could have found a drama to utilize her intelligence. M-G-M lost interest in Joan Crawford around 1938. At that point Thalberg could have found a bridge between her rags-to-riches formula and adult romances such as *Humoresque*. He could have found roles for her maturing ability and saved her from a descent into silly vehicles like *Goodbye My Fancy*.

Greta Garbo gave up her career at the peak of her powers, if this is not oversimplifying, because there was no one at M-G-M who was willing to both reassure her and guide her. Surely Thalberg could have overcome her diffidence and indecisiveness and saved her from years of inactivity. To see her in her last film, *Two-Faced Woman*, is to see coming attractions for a variety of Garbo films, all of which Thalberg could have done—

and done better. And if he could have brought Garbo to any number of classical roles, think what he could have done for Shearer, who demonstrated in *Idiot's Delight*, *The Women*, and *Escape* that she was ready for her own *Humoresque*.

There was a period after World War II when Hollywood began to make films that were as close to adult as they had been since the enforcement of the Production Code. *The Lost Weekend*, *Gilda*, *Mourning Becomes Electra*, *Gentleman's Agreement*, *Nightmare Alley*, *The Private Affairs of Bel Ami*, and *The Lady from Shanghai* were a departure from the tame fare of the previous decade. The late 1940s is the period in which Thalberg would have surpassed himself, finding great roles for Garbo and Shearer in films for which no other producer had the sensitivity and vision. Imagine Jean Harlow, Fredric March, and Norma Shearer in Thornton Wilder's *The Skin of Our Teeth*, directed by Edmund Goulding—for the I. G. Thalberg Corporation.

We can be content with the four hundred films that Thalberg did produce. In the course of writing this book, I have seen many of them for the first time, and many more for the second (or third or fourth). Would that we could see the ones that are lost. *The Divine Woman*, *The Actress*, and *London after Midnight* may turn up in some far-flung archive. When they do, we know that they will be as entertaining as *Prosperity*, as enlightening as *The Wet Parade*, and as heart-rending as *The Good Earth*. In other words, they will be as fine as every other film made by Irving Thalberg at M-G-M.